T0248245

sheet pan meals

Sheet Pan Meals

Copyright © 2024 by Cider Mill Press Book Publishers LLC.

This is an officially licensed book by Cider Mill Press Book Publishers LLC.

All rights reserved under the Pan-American and International Copyright Conventions.

No part of this book may be reproduced in whole or in part, scanned, photocopied, recorded, distributed in any printed or electronic form, or reproduced in any manner whatsoever, or by any information storage and retrieval system now known or hereafter invented, without express written permission of the publisher, except in the case of brief quotations in critical articles and reviews.

The scanning, uploading, and distribution of this book via the internet or via any other means without permission of the publisher is illegal and punishable by law. Please support authors' rights, and do not participate in or encourage piracy of copyrighted materials.

13-Digit ISBN: 978-1-40034-162-7
10-Digit ISBN: 1-40034-162-0

This book may be ordered by mail from the publisher. Please include $5.99 for postage and handling.

Please support your local bookseller first!

Books published by Cider Mill Press Book Publishers are available at special discounts for bulk purchases in the United States by corporations, institutions, and other organizations. For more information, please contact the publisher.

Cider Mill Press Book Publishers
"Where good books are ready for press"
501 Nelson Place
Nashville, Tennessee 37214

cidermillpress.com

Typography: Acumin Pro, Scotch Display Condensed
Image Credits: Photos on pages 95 and 215 used under official license from Shutterstock. All other photos courtesy of StockFood.

Printed in Malaysia
24 25 26 27 28 OFF 5 4 3 2 1
First Edition

sheet pan meals

100+ simple, delicious, hassle-free dinners

CIDER MILL PRESS

BOOK PUBLISHERS

Introduction

To everyone's dismay, the everyday world has become so demanding that there doesn't seem to be any time to actually recharge or enjoy ourselves. You get up early, drink a cup of coffee or tea, shower, get dressed, and commute to work. After working all day, you've got to get some exercise in, shower again, get home, eat something, and clean up.

And that's your day if you're doing well.

To compensate for these constraints, it's easy to start making dinner decisions that save considerable time in terms of preparation and cleanup. But we all know that, in the long run, turning to takeout night after night is too big of a trade-off in terms of our health, to say nothing of the financial outlay it requires.

To take back some of your precious time without knocking you off track in terms of wellness, it's clear that something is needed. Something miraculous.

Enter the sheet pan. With its significant surface area and incredibly versatile nature, a sheet pan is able to do the work of four or five kitchen implements all on its own, serving as a mixing bowl, large, medium, and small skillets, and even, if you have a sheet pan with high sides, a saucepan. In terms of time saved and sanity boosted, the considerable cut back on cleaning that a sheet pan provides is earth-shattering on its own. But that is only a piece of its value to the owner of an overly busy life. Because once your entree has been combined on the pan, all you have to do is slide it into the preheated oven and let the elevated temperature there transform your relatively little amount of labor into a delicious meal, with nothing more required of you than maybe a quick stir or the addition of a quicker-cooking component.

If this sounds like a cheat code that could potentially solve all of your food prep problems, you're right. A sheet pan helps you simplify without sacrificing, making it the ultimate weapon for the legion of health-conscious, time-constrained folks out there who want something delicious for dinner but don't want to spend all evening hunched over the stove and sink.

Meat

After a long day, all you want is something comforting that also allows you to recharge for the next day. Sometimes that is going to be a pepper-crusted roast beef, pork ribs, or a spicy take on sausage and peppers. Other nights it is going to be an entree where the earthy flavor of pork is balanced by the sweetness of pears and apples, or garden vegetables cutting beautifully against the rich flavor of lamb chops.

Whatever particular protein you choose, the magical sheet pan ensures that its preparation will be effortless, and the final result delicious.

Pepper-Crusted Roast Beef

6 lb. rump roast

1 teaspoon kosher salt

3 tablespoons crushed peppercorns

1 tablespoon whole-grain mustard

1 tablespoon finely chopped fresh rosemary

2 garlic cloves, crushed

¼ cup extra-virgin olive oil

1 garlic bulb, halved crosswise

2 bunches of asparagus, trimmed

2 cups cherry tomatoes

3 portobello mushrooms

2 cups Smoky Relish (see page 241), for serving

1   Preheat the oven to 400°F. Coat a sheet pan with nonstick cooking spray, place the beef in the center of the pan, and season with the salt.

2   Place the peppercorns, mustard, rosemary, garlic cloves, and half of the olive oil in a small bowl and stir to combine. Rub the mixture over the beef, place the pan in the oven, and roast the beef for 1 hour.

3   Remove the pan from the oven, add the garlic bulb, asparagus, tomatoes, and mushrooms to the pan, and drizzle the remaining olive oil over the vegetables. Return the pan to the oven and roast until the beef is medium-rare (the internal temperature is 125°F) and the vegetables are tender, 20 to 25 minutes.

4   Remove the pan from the oven, tent it loosely with aluminum foil, and let the beef rest for 20 minutes before slicing and serving with the Smoky Relish.

Pork Ribs

1 tablespoon kosher salt

2 teaspoons garlic powder

1 teaspoon onion powder

½ teaspoon black pepper

1 tablespoon chili powder

1 teaspoon paprika

¼ teaspoon cayenne pepper

2½ lbs. baby back pork ribs

1 cup BBQ sauce

1 Preheat the oven to 300°F.

2 Place the salt, garlic powder, onion powder, black pepper, chili powder, paprika, and cayenne in a small bowl and stir until combined.

3 Remove the thin membrane from the back of the ribs and rub the seasoning mixture all over the ribs. Place the ribs on a sheet pan and cover the pan tightly with aluminum foil.

4 Place the ribs in the oven and bake until they are very tender and the meat is almost falling off the bone, about 3 hours.

5 Remove the ribs from the oven. Remove the foil and generously brush the ribs with the BBQ sauce.

6 Place a rack in the upper one-third of the oven and set the broiler to high. Broil the ribs for 2 to 4 minutes, just until the sauce begins to caramelize.

7 Remove the ribs from the oven, place the foil back over the ribs, and let them rest for 10 minutes before serving.

Greek Meatballs

1 lb. ground beef

1 lb. ground lamb

1 egg

2 garlic cloves, minced

1 tablespoon dried mint

¼ cup chopped fresh parsley

½ cup almond flour

¼ cup tomato paste

1 teaspoon kosher salt

½ teaspoon black pepper

1   Preheat the oven to 375°F and line a sheet pan with parchment paper.

2   Place all of the ingredients in a large bowl and work the mixture until thoroughly combined.

3   Form tablespoons of the mixture into balls and place them on the sheet pan.

4   Place the meatballs in the oven and bake until they are cooked through and nicely browned, about 20 minutes.

5   Remove the meatballs from the oven and serve immediately.

Chorizo with Padrón Peppers & Onions

1 lb. Padrón peppers, diced

1 Vidalia onion, sliced thin

1 tablespoon extra-virgin olive oil

Salt, to taste

4 oz. fresh chorizo, sliced

1 teaspoon black pepper

½ cup sour cream

1   Preheat the oven to 425°F. Place the peppers and onion in a bowl, add the olive oil, season with salt, and toss to combine. Spread them on a sheet pan in an even layer and add the chorizo.

2   Place the pan in the oven and roast until the chorizo is cooked through and the peppers are charred all over, about 15 minutes, turning the peppers as needed.

3   Remove the pan from the oven. Stir the black pepper into the sour cream and serve it alongside the chorizo, peppers, and onion.

Pork Shoulder with Apples & Pears

5 lbs. boneless pork shoulder

2 tablespoons extra-virgin olive oil

1 tablespoon kosher salt

1 teaspoon black pepper

4 apples, cored and sliced into wedges

1 pear, cored and sliced into wedges

½ cup boiling water

2 tablespoons apple cider vinegar

2 tablespoons slivered almonds, for garnish

1 teaspoon fresh thyme, for garnish

1   Preheat the oven to 400°F. Place the pork in a sheet pan with high sides, rub it with the olive oil, and season it with the salt and pepper.

2   Place the pork in the oven and roast it for 1 hour.

3   Reduce the oven's temperature to 300°F and roast the pork for another 3 hours.

4   Remove the pan from the oven, arrange the apple and pear wedges on the pan, and pour the water and vinegar into it. Carefully return the pan to the oven and roast until the pork is tender, the exterior is crispy, and the internal temperature is 145°F.

5   Remove the pan from the oven, tent the pork with aluminum foil, and let it rest for 10 minutes. Garnish with the slivered almonds and thyme and serve.

Lamb Chops & Vegetables

2 garlic cloves, minced

1 teaspoon extra-virgin olive oil

¼ teaspoon paprika

½ teaspoon kosher salt

1 teaspoon Italian seasoning

4 lamb chops

½ cup honey

1 tablespoon apple cider vinegar

2 tablespoons Dijon mustard

2 tablespoons whole-grain mustard

1 cup Vegetable Stock (see page 233)

2 large Yukon Gold potatoes, cut into wedges

1 large carrot, peeled and chopped

2 medium zucchini, chopped

1 small yellow onion, sliced

Fresh parsley, for garnish

1 Preheat the oven to 375°F. Place the garlic, olive oil, paprika, salt, and Italian seasoning in a mixing bowl and stir to combine.

2 Place the lamb chops on a sheet pan and distribute the seasoning mixture over them.

3 Place the honey, vinegar, and mustards in a clean mixing bowl and whisk until thoroughly combined. Add the stock and whisk until incorporated.

4 Add the potatoes, carrot, zucchini, and onion to the sheet pan and pour the stock mixture over everything.

5 Cover the sheet pan with aluminum foil, place it in the oven, and bake for 20 minutes. Uncover the sheet pan and bake until the lamb chops are cooked through (the internal temperature is 125°F) and the vegetables are tender, about 10 more minutes.

6 Remove the pan from the oven and let the dish rest for 5 minutes. Garnish with fresh parsley and serve.

Pork Tenderloin with Potatoes & Vegetables

1 lb. pork tenderloin

1 lb. new potatoes

2 cups sliced bell peppers

½ red onion, cut into 1-inch chunks

¼ zucchini, halved lengthwise and sliced

3 tablespoons extra-virgin olive oil

½ teaspoon dried oregano

½ teaspoon dried parsley

1 teaspoon kosher salt

1 teaspoon black pepper

1 Preheat the oven to 400°F. Cut the pork into 8 pieces that are each about 1 inch to 1½ inches thick. Set the pork aside.

2 Place the remaining ingredients in a mixing bowl and toss to combine.

3 Place the vegetable mixture on a sheet pan in an even layer. Arrange the pork on top and place the pan in the oven.

4 Roast until the pork is cooked through (the internal temperature should be about 145°F) and the potatoes are tender, about 30 minutes.

5 Remove the pan from the oven and serve.

Pork Chops & Turkey Meatballs

For the Meatballs

1 lb. ground turkey

1 teaspoon cumin

1 teaspoon paprika

1 teaspoon dried oregano

Salt and pepper, to taste

For the Pork Chops

1 teaspoon cumin seeds

¼ teaspoon cinnamon

Pinch of cayenne pepper

½ teaspoon kosher salt

¼ teaspoon black pepper

2 teaspoons brown sugar

1 tablespoon extra-virgin olive oil

4 bone-in pork chops

1 red apple, cored and cut into wedges

1 Bosc pear, cored and cut into slivers

1 bunch of broccolini, trimmed

Fresh parsley, chopped, for garnish

Brown gravy, for serving (optional)

1 Preheat the oven to 400°F. Line a sheet pan with aluminum foil.

2 To prepare the meatballs, place all of the ingredients in a mixing bowl and work the mixture with your hands until thoroughly combined. Form the mixture into 1-inch balls and arrange them on half of the sheet pan.

3 To begin preparations for the pork chops, place the cumin seeds, cinnamon, cayenne pepper, salt, black pepper, brown sugar, and olive oil in a mixing bowl and stir to combine.

4 Place the pork chops on the other half of the sheet pan and drizzle the brown sugar mixture over them.

5 Arrange the apple, pear, and broccolini around the meatballs and pork chops. Place the pan in the oven and roast until the meatballs and pork chops are browned and cooked through, 20 to 25 minutes, turning the sheet pan halfway through.

6 Remove the pan from the oven and let the dish rest for 2 to 3 minutes. Garnish with fresh parsley and serve with brown gravy, if desired.

Lamb with Chimichurri & Grilled Lemon Asparagus

For the Lamb

5 lb. bone-in leg of lamb

1 tablespoon extra-virgin olive oil

2 teaspoons kosher salt

1 teaspoon black pepper

For the Asparagus

3 lemons, halved

2 bunches of asparagus, trimmed

2 tablespoons extra-virgin olive oil

1 teaspoon kosher salt

¼ teaspoon black pepper

Chimichurri Sauce
(see page 240)

1   To begin preparations for the lamb, preheat the oven to 325°F. Set a wire rack in a sheet pan and place the lamb on the rack, fat side up. Brush the lamb with the olive oil, season it with the salt and pepper, and place it in the oven. Roast until the lamb is medium-rare, about 2½ hours.

2   While the lamb is in the oven, begin preparations for the asparagus. Prepare a gas or charcoal grill for high heat (about 500°F). Place the lemons on the grill, cut side down, and grill until they are charred, 3 to 5 minutes. Remove the lemons from the grill and set them aside.

3   Remove the lamb from the oven and let it rest for 15 minutes. Raise the oven's temperature to 425°F.

4   Place the asparagus on a sheet pan, drizzle the olive oil over it, and season with the salt and pepper. Toss to combine, arrange the asparagus in an even layer, and squeeze half of the grilled lemons over it.

5   Place the asparagus in the oven and roast until it is tender, about 12 minutes.

6   While the asparagus is in the oven, slice the remaining grilled lemons and set them aside.

7   Remove the asparagus from the oven. Slice the lamb and serve it with the asparagus, topping each portion with some chimichurri and slices of grilled lemon.

Pork with Roasted Root Vegetables

3 parsnips, peeled and cut into large chunks

4 large carrots, peeled and cut into large chunks

1 lb. new potatoes, cut into large chunks

2 tablespoons extra-virgin olive oil

2 teaspoons kosher salt

3 red onions, cut into wedges

2 apples, cored and cut into wedges

1½ lbs. pork tenderloin, cut into 8 pieces

1 teaspoon freshly ground black pepper

1 Preheat the oven to 425°F. Place the parsnips, carrots, and potatoes in a mixing bowl, add the olive oil and half of the salt, and toss to combine. Place the vegetables on a sheet pan, place them in the oven, and roast for 30 minutes.

2 Remove the pan from the oven and stir in the onions and apples. Season the pork with the remaining salt and the pepper, add it to the sheet pan, and return the pan to the oven.

3 Roast until the pork is cooked through (the internal temperature is about 145°F), about 20 minutes.

4 Remove the pan from the oven and let the dish rest for 2 to 3 minutes before serving.

Yield: 8 Servings | Active Time: 25 Minutes | Total Time: 24 Hours

Lamb with Anchovy & Mint Yogurt

2 cups Greek yogurt

4 garlic cloves, crushed

½ cup fresh mint, plus more for garnish

2 teaspoons dried oregano

2 teaspoons cumin

1 teaspoon coriander

6 anchovies in olive oil, drained

3 tablespoons fresh lemon juice

5 lbs. boneless lamb shoulder

1 tablespoon kosher salt

1 teaspoon black pepper

2 tablespoons extra-virgin olive oil

2 cups cherry tomatoes, for garnish

1   Place the yogurt, garlic, mint, oregano, cumin, coriander, anchovies, and lemon juice in a food processor and pulse until the mixture is smooth and combined. Place the lamb in a nonreactive dish and pour the marinade over it. Cover the dish and let the lamb marinate in the refrigerator overnight.

2   Preheat the oven to 450°F. Remove the lamb from marinade, transfer it to a sheet pan, season it with the salt and pepper, and drizzle the olive oil over the top.

3   Place the lamb in the oven and roast until the internal temperature is about 125°F, about 1½ hours.

4   Remove the lamb from the oven, tent it loosely with aluminum foil, and let it rest for 15 minutes before slicing.

5   Place the tomatoes on a sheet pan and set the oven's broiler to high. Place the tomatoes under the broiler and broil until they start to burst and char, 6 to 8 minutes. Remove the tomatoes from the oven, serve them alongside the lamb, and garnish with additional mint.

Mediterranean Lamb Chops

2 tablespoons extra-virgin olive oil

8 lamb loin chops, trimmed

1 large potato, sliced thin

1 red onion, cut into wedges

1 tablespoon fresh lemon thyme

¼ cup Chicken Stock (see page 234)

1 red bell pepper, stem and seeds removed, sliced

1 small yellow pepper, stem and seeds removed, sliced

1 lemon, cut into wedges

2 garlic cloves, sliced

1 teaspoon kosher salt

½ teaspoon black pepper

¾ lb. cherry tomatoes

⅓ cup pitted Kalamata olives

½ cup crumbled feta cheese

Fresh thyme, for garnish

1   Preheat the oven to 400°F. Place the olive oil in a large skillet and warm it over high heat. Add the lamb and sear it for 2 minutes on each side. Remove the lamb from the pan, cover it with aluminum foil, and set it aside.

2   Place the potato, onion, lemon thyme, and stock in a sheet pan with high sides and stir. Place the pan in the oven and bake until the onion is almost tender, about 15 minutes.

3   Remove the pan from the oven and add the peppers, lemon wedges, and garlic. Stir gently to combine, season with the salt and pepper, and top with the tomatoes. Return the pan to the oven and bake until the vegetables are almost tender, about 15 minutes.

4   Remove the pan from the oven and arrange the seared lamb chops on top of the vegetable mixture. Sprinkle the olives and feta over the dish and return it to the oven. Bake until the lamb is just cooked through (the internal temperature is 125°F) and the vegetables are beginning to char, about 10 minutes.

5   Remove the pan from the oven, garnish the dish with thyme, and serve.

Veal Caprese

2 large eggs

3 cups Italian seasoned bread crumbs

6 veal cutlets, pounded to ⅛ inch thick

3 tablespoons unsalted butter

¼ cup extra-virgin olive oil

1 teaspoon kosher salt

½ teaspoon black pepper

1 cup Pesto (see page 235)

1 heirloom tomato, sliced

½ lb. mozzarella cheese, cut into thick slices

1 handful of fresh basil

1   Preheat the oven to 400°F. Place the eggs in a bowl and whisk until scrambled. Place the bread crumbs in a shallow bowl. Dredge the veal in the eggs and then in the bread crumbs until it is coated all over. Set the breaded veal aside.

2   Place the butter and olive oil on a sheet pan, place the pan in the oven, and melt the butter. Carefully remove the pan from the oven and gently tilt the pan to spread the butter and olive oil over it evenly.

3   Arrange the breaded veal in the pan, season with the salt and pepper, and return the pan to the oven. Bake for 15 minutes, turning the veal over halfway through.

4   Remove the pan from the oven and set the oven's broiler to high. Spread the Pesto over the veal and arrange the tomato and mozzarella around it. Top with half of the basil leaves and return the pan to the oven.

5   Broil until the veal is completely cooked through and the mozzarella has melted, about 5 minutes.

6   Remove the pan from the oven, top the dish with the remaining basil, and serve.

Yield: 4 Servings | Active Time: 25 Minutes | Total Time: 1 Hour and 5 Minutes

Prosciutto, Mushroom & Artichoke Frittata

½ lb. cremini mushrooms, sliced

1 tablespoon extra-virgin olive oil

8 eggs

1 cup milk

2 garlic cloves, minced

1 cup grated Parmesan cheese

Black pepper, to taste

2 cups cherry tomatoes

1 cup halved artichoke hearts

4 oz. prosciutto, sliced

1 cup baby arugula, for garnish

Fresh basil, for garnish

1   Preheat the oven to 400°F. Coat a sheet pan with high sides with parchment paper.

2   Place the mushrooms in the pan and drizzle the olive oil over them. Place them in the oven and roast until they start to brown, 5 to 8 minutes.

3   While the mushrooms are in the oven, place the eggs, milk, and garlic in a large bowl and whisk to combine. Stir in half of the Parmesan and season with pepper.

4   Remove the pan from the oven and carefully pour the egg mixture into the pan. Arrange the tomatoes and artichokes in the egg mixture and return the pan to the oven.

5   Bake until the eggs have set, about 25 minutes.

6   Remove the pan from the oven and place the prosciutto on top of the frittata in an even layer. Return the pan to the oven and bake until the prosciutto is golden brown and crispy, about 10 minutes.

7   Remove the sheet pan from the oven, garnish the frittata with the arugula and basil, and serve.

Tangy BBQ Ribs

8 garlic cloves, minced

1 small yellow onion, finely diced

4 teaspoons kosher salt

1 teaspoon black pepper

1 tablespoon German mustard

1 tablespoon Worcestershire sauce

1 teaspoon dried oregano

¼ teaspoon cumin

1 teaspoon cayenne pepper

¼ cup apple cider vinegar

1 cup crushed tomatoes

2 lbs. pork spareribs, trimmed

Fresh rosemary, for garnish

1   Place the garlic, onion, salt, pepper, mustard, Worcestershire sauce, oregano, cumin, cayenne, vinegar, and crushed tomatoes in a mixing bowl and stir until well combined.

2   Place the spareribs on a large sheet pan, spread three-quarters of the sauce over the ribs, and then let them marinate in the refrigerator for 1 hour. Reserve the remaining sauce.

3   Preheat the oven to 350°F. Cover the sheet pan tightly with aluminum foil, place it in the oven, and bake until the spareribs are tender, about 1½ hours.

4   Set the oven's broiler to high, remove the foil, and discard it. Broil the ribs until the sauce has caramelized, about 5 minutes.

5   Remove the pan from the oven and let the ribs rest for 10 minutes before serving. Garnish the ribs with rosemary and serve with the reserved sauce.

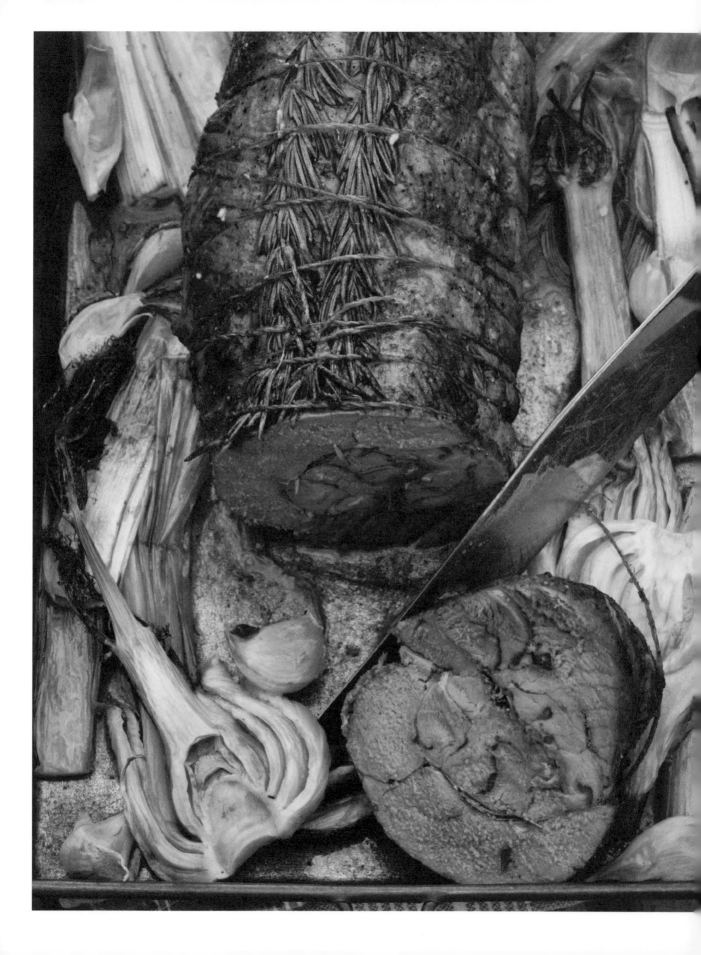

Garlic & Herb Lamb

2 tablespoons extra-virgin olive oil

1½ teaspoons garlic salt

1 tablespoon Dijon mustard

2 tablespoons finely chopped fresh rosemary

2 lbs. boneless leg of lamb, butterflied

Handful of fresh mint

1 tablespoon kosher salt

2 bulbs of fennel, trimmed and halved

Cloves from 1 bulb of garlic

1   Preheat the oven to 375°F. Place 1 tablespoon of olive oil, the garlic salt, and mustard in a mixing bowl and stir to combine. Stir in one-quarter of the rosemary.

2   Spread half of the olive oil mixture over the inside of the lamb and top it with the mint and one-quarter of the rosemary. Close up the lamb, rub the remaining olive oil mixture over the exterior of the lamb, sprinkle the remaining rosemary over the top, and then tie the lamb with kitchen twine.

3   Place the lamb on a sheet pan, season with half of the kosher salt, and place it in the oven. Roast for 30 minutes.

4   Remove the pan from the oven and add the fennel and garlic. Drizzle the remaining olive oil over the vegetables and season with the remaining kosher salt. Return the pan to the oven and roast until the lamb is cooked through (the internal temperature is 125°F to 130°F) and the fennel is tender.

5   Remove the pan from the oven, tent it loosely with aluminum foil, and let the lamb rest for 10 to 15 minutes before slicing and serving.

Pork Chops with Eggplant & Rhubarb

1 tablespoon mirin

1 tablespoon sesame oil

2 tablespoons canola oil

3 tablespoons soy sauce

1 tablespoon rice vinegar

½ teaspoon black pepper

¼ teaspoon coriander seeds

2 Japanese eggplants, halved lengthwise

4 bone-in pork chops (each 1½ to 2 inches thick)

¼ cup sliced rhubarb

Fresh thyme, for garnish

1. Set the oven's broiler to high. Place the mirin, sesame oil, canola oil, soy sauce, vinegar, pepper, and coriander seeds in a bowl and stir to combine.

2. Arrange the eggplants and pork on a sheet pan. Add the rhubarb and pour the sauce over the dish, making sure the pork is completely coated.

3. Place the sheet pan in the oven and broil for 8 minutes. Turn the pork over and cook until it is cooked through (the internal temperature is 140°F).

4. Remove the pan from the oven, cover it loosely with aluminum foil, and let the dish rest for 5 minutes. Garnish with thyme and serve.

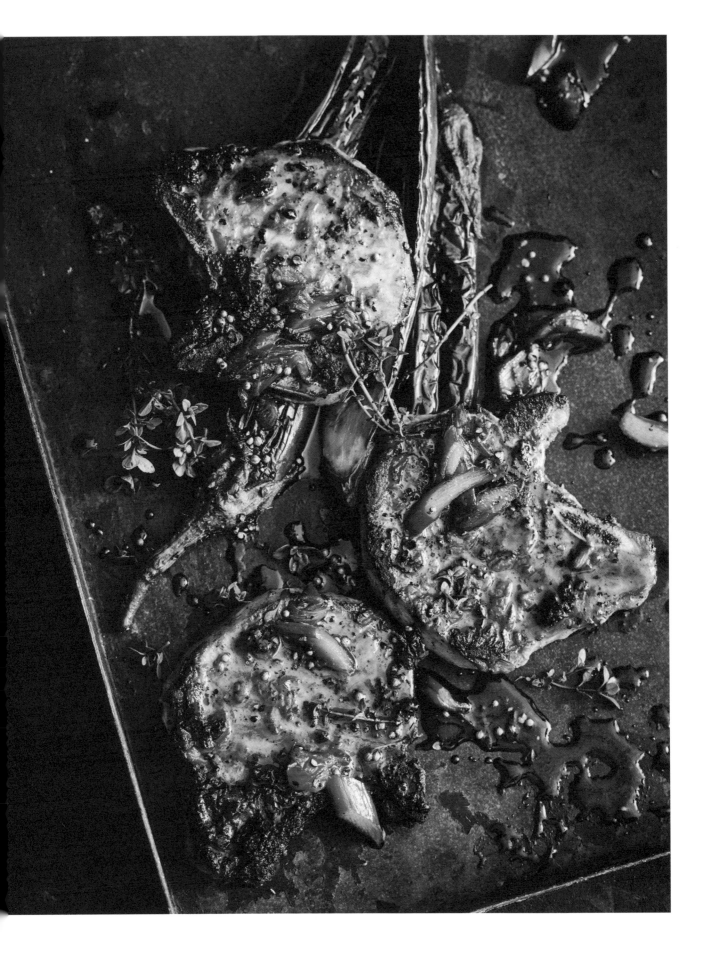

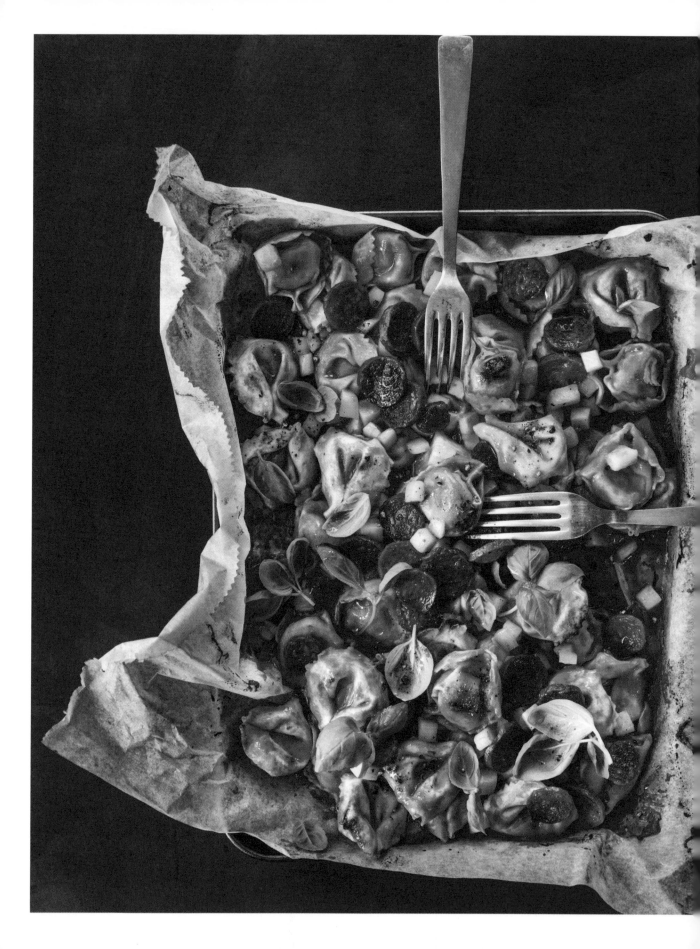

Tortelloni with Chorizo and Mango & Tomato Sauce

1 (14 oz.) can of stewed tomatoes, drained and chopped

Flesh of ½ small mango, diced

4 oz. chorizo, sliced

1 teaspoon kosher salt

1 teaspoon black pepper

1¼ lbs. tortelloni

Fresh basil, for garnish

1　Preheat the oven to 400°F. Line a sheet pan with parchment paper.

2　Place all of the ingredients, except for the basil, on the sheet pan and stir to combine.

3　Place the pan in the oven and bake until the tortelloni are al dente, about 15 minutes. Remove the pan from the oven, garnish the dish with basil, and serve.

Roasted Vegetables & Sausages

2 large sweet potatoes, cut into wedges

2 waxy potatoes, cut into wedges

6 pork sausages, pricked with a fork

½ lb. cherry tomatoes

1 large red onion, cut into wedges

1 green pepper, stem and seeds removed, sliced

¼ cup extra-virgin olive oil

2 teaspoons finely chopped fresh oregano

1 teaspoon finely chopped fresh rosemary

Salt and pepper, to taste

1 lemon, halved

1   Preheat the oven to 400°F.

2   Place all of the ingredients, except for the lemon, in a mixing bowl and toss to combine. Transfer the mixture to a sheet pan and place it in the oven.

3   Roast until the sausages are cooked through and the vegetables are tender and browned, about 45 minutes, rotating the pan halfway through.

4   Remove the pan from the oven and let the dish cool briefly. Squeeze the lemon over the top and serve.

Yield: 2 Servings | Active Time: 20 Minutes | Total Time: 55 Minutes

Pork Collar Steaks with Onions & Potatoes

¼ cup sliced onions (mix of red and yellow)

1 cup quartered new potatoes

1 tablespoon olive oil

1½ teaspoons kosher salt

1 teaspoon black pepper

2 boneless center-cut pork shoulder steaks

1 tablespoon herbes de Provençe

1   Preheat the oven to 400°F. Line a sheet pan with parchment paper. Place the onions and potatoes on the pan, drizzle half of the olive oil over the vegetables, and season with half of the salt and half of the pepper. Place the pan in the oven and roast for 10 minutes.

2   Remove the pan from the oven and place the pork steaks on top of the vegetables. Drizzle the remaining olive oil over the dish, season with the remaining salt and pepper, and sprinkle the herbes de Provençe over the dish. Toss to coat and return the pan to the oven.

3   Roast until the pork is cooked through (the internal temperature is 145°F) and the vegetables are tender, 20 to 25 minutes.

4   Remove the pan from the oven and let the dish rest for 5 minutes before serving.

Yield: 2 Servings | Active Time: 30 Minutes | Total Time: 50 Minutes

Spiedino Kebabs

½ yellow bell pepper, cut into 1-inch squares

½ red bell pepper, cut into 1-inch squares

1 large boneless, skinless chicken breast, cut into 1-inch chunks

½ lb. skinless pork belly, cut into 1-inch chunks

6 slices of baguette

2 tablespoons extra-virgin olive oil

½ teaspoon kosher salt

1 tablespoon cracked black peppercorns

1 tablespoon finely chopped fresh rosemary

1 Preheat the oven to 450°F.

2 Thread the bell peppers, chicken, pork belly, and baguette onto skewers, alternating between them. Place them on a sheet pan, drizzle the olive oil over them, and season with the salt, peppercorns, and rosemary.

3 Toss to coat and place the pan in the oven. Bake until the chicken and pork belly are cooked through and the baguette is golden brown, about 20 minutes.

4 Remove the pan from the oven and serve immediately.

Pork Chops with Fingerling Potatoes & Brussels Sprouts

2 teaspoons kosher salt

½ teaspoon black pepper

½ teaspoon garlic powder

¼ teaspoon onion powder

½ teaspoon chili powder

2 tablespoons brown sugar

2 bone-in pork chops

¼ cup extra-virgin olive oil

1½ lbs. fingerling potatoes, quartered lengthwise

2 cups trimmed Brussels sprouts

Fresh sage, chopped, for garnish

1   Preheat the oven to 400°F. Place half of the salt, half of the pepper, the garlic powder, onion powder, chili powder, and brown sugar in a mixing bowl and stir until thoroughly combined.

2   Place the pork chops on a sheet pan and coat both sides with half of the olive oil. Sprinkle half of the seasoning mixture over the pork chops and rub it into the meat. Turn the pork chops over and repeat with the remaining seasoning mixture.

3   Place the potatoes and Brussels sprouts in a bowl, add the remaining olive oil, salt, and pepper, and toss to coat. Transfer the vegetables to the sheet pan and arrange them around the pork chops.

4   Place the pan in the oven and roast for 15 minutes.

5   Turn the pork chops over and roast until they are cooked through (the internal temperature is 145°F) and the vegetables are tender, about 20 minutes.

6   Remove the pan from the oven and let the dish rest for a few minutes. Garnish with sage and serve.

Leg of Lamb with Carrots & Potatoes

2 garlic cloves, minced

3 tablespoons extra-virgin olive oil

1 tablespoon Dijon mustard

1 tablespoon finely chopped fresh rosemary

½ tablespoon finely chopped fresh oregano, plus more for garnish

2 teaspoons kosher salt

1 teaspoon black pepper

5 to 6 lb. bone-in leg of lamb

1 lb. new potatoes, cut into wedges

1 lb. baby carrots, quartered lengthwise

4 shallots, peeled and halved

1 Preheat the oven to 450°F. Place a sheet pan in the oven and let it heat up as the oven warms.

2 Place the garlic, 2 tablespoons of olive oil, the mustard, rosemary, oregano, half of the salt, and half of the pepper in a small bowl and stir to combine. Generously apply the mixture to the lamb, place the lamb on the pan in the oven, and roast for 10 minutes.

3 Reduce the oven's temperature to 350°F and roast the lamb for another 30 minutes.

4 While the lamb is in the oven, place the potatoes, carrots, and shallots in a large bowl, add the remaining olive oil, salt, and pepper, and toss to coat.

5 Remove the pan from the oven. Arrange the potatoes, carrots, and shallots around the lamb and place the pan back in the oven. Roast until the lamb is cooked through (the internal temperature is 125°F) and the vegetables are tender, 30 to 40 minutes.

6 Remove the pan from the oven and let the dish rest for 10 minutes. Garnish with additional oregano and serve.

Pork Kebabs with Anchovy Sauce

6 long, thick sprigs of fresh rosemary

2 tablespoons finely chopped fresh rosemary

Juice of 2 lemons

1 garlic clove, minced

10 anchovy fillets

⅓ cup plus 1 tablespoon olive oil

2 lbs. boneless pork neck, cut into 1-inch cubes

3 baby fennel bulbs, cut into wedges

18 fresh bay leaves

1 teaspoon kosher salt

½ teaspoon black pepper

1. Preheat the oven to 400°F. Remove the rosemary leaves from the sprigs and sharpen one end of each sprig to a point with a knife. Set the rosemary skewers aside.

2. Use a mortar and pestle to grind the finely chopped rosemary and 1 tablespoon of lemon juice into a coarse paste. Add the garlic and anchovies and grind the mixture into a thick, smooth paste. Gradually add ⅓ cup of olive oil and the remaining lemon juice and grind until the olive oil has emulsified. Transfer the sauce to a small serving bowl and set it aside.

3. Thread the pork, fennel, and bay leaves onto the skewers, alternating between them. Drizzle the remaining olive oil over the skewers, season with the salt and pepper, and place them on a sheet pan.

4. Place the pan in the oven and bake until the pork is cooked through and the fennel is tender, about 15 minutes, turning the skewers once or twice.

5. Set the oven's broiler to high and broil until the pork is lightly charred, about 5 minutes. Remove the pan from the oven and serve immediately with the anchovy sauce.

Meatball Skewers

1¼ lbs. ground beef

1 teaspoon dried oregano

½ teaspoon dried basil

Pinch of red pepper flakes

Salt and pepper, to taste

6 slices of bacon, halved

1 small red bell pepper, stem and seeds removed, cut into large squares

1 small yellow bell pepper, stem and seeds removed, cut into large squares

4 cherry tomatoes, halved

½ lb. fresh mozzarella cheese, drained and cut into large chunks

1 small baguette, cut into thin slices

2 tablespoons extra-virgin olive oil

1   Preheat the oven to 400°F. Place the ground beef, dried herbs, and red pepper flakes in a mixing bowl, generously season with salt and pepper, and work the mixture until thoroughly combined. Form the mixture into 12 meatballs.

2   Thread the meatballs, bacon, peppers, tomatoes, mozzarella, and bread onto skewers, alternating between them and folding the bacon as needed to make it fit.

3   Place the skewers on a sheet pan and drizzle the olive oil over them. Season with salt and pepper and place the pan in the oven.

4   Roast the skewers until the meatballs are cooked through and the vegetables are lightly charred, about 20 minutes, turning them over as needed.

5   Remove the pan from the oven and let the skewers cool briefly before serving.

Pork Schnitzel with Brussels Sprouts & Frites

2 Yukon Gold potatoes, cut into ¼-inch fries

1 lb. Brussels sprouts, trimmed and halved

3 tablespoons extra-virgin olive oil

1 tablespoon finely chopped fresh rosemary

2 teaspoons kosher salt

Black pepper, to taste

¼ cup almond flour

2 eggs

1 cup crumbled cornflakes

2 boneless pork chops (each 1 inch thick)

2 oz. Gruyère cheese, grated

1   Preheat the oven to 425°F. Line a sheet pan with parchment paper.

2   Place the potatoes and Brussels sprouts in a mixing bowl, add the olive oil, rosemary, and half of the salt, and season with pepper. Toss to coat and transfer the mixture to the sheet pan, arranging it in an even layer. Place the pan in the oven and roast the vegetables for 15 minutes.

3   Place the flour, eggs, and cornflakes in three separate shallow bowls. Beat the eggs until scrambled and season the pork chops with the remaining salt. Dredge the pork chops in the flour, eggs, and cornflakes until they are completely coated.

4   Remove the pan from the oven and place the breaded pork chops on the pan. Return the pan to the oven and roast for about 10 minutes.

5   Remove the pan from the oven and sprinkle the Gruyère over the vegetables. Return the pan to the oven and roast until the pork chops are golden brown and cooked through (the internal temperature is 145°F) and the cheese has melted, 5 to 10 minutes.

6   Remove the pan from the oven and serve immediately.

Yield: 4 Servings | Active Time: 40 Minutes | Total Time: 1 Hour and 40 Minutes

Rabbit with Rhubarb Compote

¼ cup honey

3 tablespoons extra-virgin olive oil

1½ cups Chicken Stock (see page 234)

1 teaspoon coriander seeds, crushed

1 teaspoon kosher salt

½ teaspoon black pepper

4 rabbit legs

½ lb. fingerling potatoes, halved

2 shallots, halved lengthwise

2 rhubarb stalks, trimmed and quartered

1 lb. baby carrots, trimmed and halved lengthwise

2 slices of ruby red grapefruit

1 star anise pod

Fresh oregano, for garnish

Fig & Rhubarb Compote (see page 244), for serving

1   Preheat the oven to 400°F. Place the honey, olive oil, stock, coriander seeds, salt, and pepper in a mixing bowl and stir to combine.

2   Place the rabbit in a sheet pan with high sides and pour the honey mixture over the top. Place the pan in the oven and bake for 40 minutes.

3   Remove the pan from the oven and add the potatoes, shallots, rhubarb, carrots, grapefruit, and star anise pod. Baste the rabbit with the pan juices and return the pan to the oven.

4   Bake until the rabbit is cooked through (the internal temperature is 160°F) and the vegetables are tender, 20 to 25 minutes.

5   Remove the pan from the oven, garnish the dish with oregano, and serve it with the Fig & Rhubarb Compote.

Yield: 4 Servings | Active Time: 25 Minutes | Total Time: 1 Hour and 5 Minutes

Kielbasa & Eggs

1 lb. potatoes, diced into ½-inch cubes

1 orange bell pepper, diced into ½-inch squares

1 small red onion, sliced

1 lb. kielbasa, diced into ½-inch cubes

2 tablespoons extra-virgin olive oil

1 teaspoon kosher salt

Black pepper, to taste

4 eggs

Fresh parsley, chopped, for garnish

1   Preheat the oven to 400°F. Place the potatoes, bell pepper, onion, and kielbasa in a mixing bowl, drizzle the olive oil over the mixture, and season with the salt and pepper. Toss to coat and spread the mixture in an even layer on a sheet pan.

2   Place the pan in the oven and bake for 30 minutes.

3   Remove the pan from the oven, make four wells in the mixture, and crack an egg into each, making sure to keep the yolks intact.

4   Return the pan to the oven and bake until the egg whites are set, about 10 minutes.

5   Remove the pan from the oven, garnish the dish with parsley, and serve.

Poultry

Everyone knows that poultry is a great option when you're looking for something to build an entree around, as its neutral flavor allows it to play well with a number of elements.

But that relative lack of flavor can also cause chicken, turkey, and duck to become a bit grating to those who turn to it time after time, a characteristic that makes it easy to start looking past. Fortunately, the ease of the sheet pan makes poultry impossible to ignore, and the irresistible touch that roasting it in the high heat of an oven adds is another encouraging element. We've also traversed the globe and plucked the very best seasoning blends, marinades, and sauces from various cuisines to guarantee that there's no rolling of the eyes when poultry is what's on the menu.

Yield: 4 Servings | Active Time: 30 Minutes | Total Time: 4 Hours and 20 Minutes

Jerk Chicken

4 garlic cloves, smashed

1 habanero chile pepper, stem and seeds removed, finely diced

1 tablespoon grated fresh ginger

¼ cup fresh lime juice

¼ cup soy sauce

1½ tablespoons brown sugar

1 teaspoon black pepper

1 teaspoon allspice

½ teaspoon cinnamon

½ teaspoon freshly grated nutmeg

8 bone-in, skin-on chicken thighs and legs

1 onion, sliced

2 limes, halved

Fresh thyme, for garnish

1   Place the garlic, habanero, ginger, lime juice, soy sauce, brown sugar, black pepper, allspice, cinnamon, and nutmeg in a mixing bowl and whisk until thoroughly combined.

2   Place the chicken in a large resealable bag. Pour the marinade into the bag, seal it, and gently shake. Marinate the chicken in the refrigerator for 3 hours.

3   Preheat the oven to 375°F. Place the chicken and marinade in a sheet pan with high sides. Arrange the onion and limes between the chicken pieces.

4   Place the pan in the oven and roast until it is cooked through, 45 to 50 minutes.

5   Set the oven's broiler to high and broil the chicken for 5 minutes.

6   Remove the pan from the oven and let the chicken rest for 5 minutes. Garnish with fresh thyme and serve.

Yield: 4 to 6 Servings | Active Time: 25 Minutes | Total Time: 4 Hours and 25 Minutes

Cornish Game Hens with Pomegranate

¼ cup extra-virgin olive oil

2 tablespoons pomegranate molasses

1 teaspoon za'atar

1 teaspoon paprika

1 teaspoon garlic powder

½ teaspoon dried oregano

½ teaspoon kosher salt

½ teaspoon black pepper

4 Cornish game hens, butterflied

1 shallot, sliced

1 lemon, sliced

4 cinnamon sticks

¼ cup pomegranate arils

1   Line a sheet pan that will fit in your refrigerator with parchment paper. Place the olive oil, pomegranate molasses, za'atar, paprika, garlic powder, oregano, salt, and pepper in a mixing bowl and stir to combine.

2   Lay the Cornish game hens on the sheet pan and coat them with the seasoned oil. Scatter the shallot and lemon slices around the Cornish game hens, cover the pan tightly with aluminum foil, and let the Cornish game hens marinate in the refrigerator for at least 3 hours.

3   Remove the Cornish game hens from the refrigerator and preheat the oven to 400°F. Add the cinnamon sticks to the sheet pan and sprinkle the pomegranate arils over the Cornish game hens.

4   Place the sheet pan in the oven and bake until the Cornish game hens are cooked through (their internal temperature should be 165°F), 50 minutes to 1 hour.

5   Set the oven's broiler to high and broil the Cornish game hens until their skin is crispy. Remove the pan from the oven and let the Cornish game hens rest for 5 minutes before serving.

Fennel & Citrus Chicken Thighs

2 teaspoons fennel seeds

2 garlic cloves, chopped

Zest and juice of ½ orange

Zest and juice of ½ lemon

8 chicken thighs

1 teaspoon kosher salt

½ teaspoon black pepper

2 tablespoons extra-virgin olive oil

8 baby fennel bulbs, trimmed, fronds reserved for garnish

1 orange, sliced

1 grapefruit, sliced

1 lemon, sliced

1   Preheat the oven to 350°F. Use a mortar and pestle to grind the fennel seeds, garlic, and citrus zests. Season the chicken with the salt and pepper and the fennel seed mixture and drizzle the olive oil over it.

2   Arrange the fennel bulbs and citrus slices on a sheet pan. Add the chicken to the pan and pour the orange juice and lemon juice over the dish.

3   Place the pan in the oven and roast until the chicken is cooked through (the internal temperature is 165°F), about 15 minutes, basting the chicken halfway through.

4   Remove the chicken from the oven, garnish with the fennel fronds, and serve.

Spatchcock Chicken in Turmeric & Coconut Sauce

4½ lb. whole chicken, spatchcocked

1 tablespoon kosher salt

1 teaspoon black pepper

4 tablespoons unsalted butter, softened

1½ lbs. new potatoes, halved

3 red onions, quartered

1 (14 oz.) can of coconut milk

1 cup Chicken Stock (see page 234)

3 tablespoons fresh lemon juice

1 tablespoon ground turmeric

2 teaspoons coriander

2 teaspoons cumin

1 teaspoon black mustard seeds

1 tablespoon freshly grated turmeric

1 cup trimmed French green beans

Fresh cilantro, for garnish

1. Preheat the oven to 400°F. Place the chicken in a sheet pan with high sides. Season the chicken with the salt and pepper and rub the skin with the butter. Arrange the potatoes and onions around the chicken.

2. Place the coconut milk, stock, lemon juice, ground turmeric, coriander, cumin, mustard seeds, and grated turmeric in a bowl and whisk until thoroughly combined. Pour the sauce into the pan.

3. Place the pan in the oven and roast until the chicken is cooked through (the internal temperature is about 160°F) and the skin is golden brown, about 1 hour.

4. Remove the sheet pan from the oven, add the green beans, and return the pan to the oven. Bake until the green beans are tender, about 10 minutes.

5. Remove the pan from the oven, garnish with fresh cilantro, and serve.

Honey & Turmeric Chicken Thighs with Olives

8 bone-in, skin-on chicken thighs and drumsticks

Salt and pepper, to taste

Zest and juice of 2 lemons

3 tablespoons extra-virgin olive oil

2 teaspoons turmeric

1 teaspoon ground ginger

1 tablespoon honey

1 cup dry white wine

Cloves from 1 head of garlic, chopped

2 tablespoons capers

½ cup pitted mixed olives

¼ cup raisins

3 bay leaves

Fresh parsley, chopped, for garnish

1 Preheat the oven to 350°F. Place the chicken in a sheet pan with high sides in an even layer and season it with salt and pepper.

2 Add all of the remaining ingredients, except for the parsley, and stir to combine.

3 Place the chicken in the oven and roast until it is cooked through (the internal temperature is about 165°F), about 1 hour.

4 Remove the pan from the oven, garnish the dish with the fresh parsley, and serve.

Yogurt-Marinated Chicken with Spicy Chickpeas

1½ cups Greek yogurt

5 tablespoons fresh lemon juice

2 teaspoons turmeric

2 tablespoons water

3 to 4 lbs. bone-in, skin-on chicken pieces

Salt and pepper, to taste

2 (14 oz.) cans of chickpeas, drained and rinsed

1 tablespoon fennel seeds

1 teaspoon cumin

1 large red onion, sliced thin

2 tablespoons extra-virgin olive oil

Fresh mint, chopped, for garnish

Fresh cilantro, chopped, for garnish

1   Place ¾ cup of yogurt, 2 tablespoons of lemon juice, 1 teaspoon of turmeric, and the water in a large bowl and stir to combine. Add the chicken, season generously with salt and pepper, and toss to coat evenly. Cover the bowl and let the chicken marinate in the refrigerator overnight.

2   Preheat the oven to 425°F. Place the chickpeas, fennel seeds, cumin, remaining turmeric, and half of the red onion on a sheet pan, drizzle the olive oil over the mixture, season with salt and pepper, and toss to coat.

3   Move the chickpeas to the outer edges of the pan. Scrape any excess marinade off the chicken and arrange it in the center of the sheet pan. Place in the oven and bake, stirring the chickpeas occasionally, until the chicken is cooked through (the internal temperature is 165°F) and the chickpeas are golden brown and starting to become crispy, 45 to 50 minutes.

4   While the chicken and chickpeas are in the oven, place the remaining onion and 2 tablespoons of lemon juice in a bowl, season with salt and pepper, and toss to combine. Set the mixture aside. Combine the remaining yogurt with the remaining lemon juice, season with salt and pepper, and stir to combine.

5   Remove the chicken from the oven and top the dish with the lightly pickled onion. Garnish with mint and cilantro and serve with the seasoned yogurt.

Yield: 2 to 4 Servings | Active Time: 25 Minutes | Total Time: 1 Hour

Harissa Chicken with Potatoes, Fennel & Leeks

4 skin-on chicken thighs

1 lb. new potatoes, quartered

2 leeks, halved lengthwise, rinsed well, and sliced thin

2 fennel bulbs, trimmed and cut into wedges, fronds reserved for garnish

1 teaspoon kosher salt

1 tablespoon extra-virgin olive oil

1 teaspoon harissa paste

4 garlic cloves, crushed

2 tablespoons fresh lemon juice

1   Preheat the oven to 400°F and coat a sheet pan with nonstick cooking spray.

2   Place all of the ingredients, except for the fennel fronds, in a mixing bowl and toss until well combined.

3   Place the mixture on the pan in an even layer. Place it in the oven and bake until the chicken is cooked through (the internal temperature is 165°F), 35 to 40 minutes.

4   Remove the pan from the oven, garnish the dish with the fennel fronds, and serve.

Chicken Saltimbocca

1 lb. boneless, skinless chicken breasts

1 teaspoon kosher salt

½ teaspoon black pepper

12 fresh sage leaves

8 slices of prosciutto

Cloves from 1 garlic bulb, separated and unpeeled

½ lemon, cut into wedges

1 tablespoon extra-virgin olive oil

1 cup red grapes

1   Preheat the oven to 425°F. Coat a sheet pan with nonstick cooking spray.

2   Season the chicken breasts with the salt and pepper, lay 2 sage leaves on top of each chicken breast, and then wrap each one with 2 slices of prosciutto, covering the entire breast.

3   Carefully place the chicken on the pan and arrange the garlic cloves around it. Squeeze the lemon over the chicken and drizzle the olive oil over it.

4   Scatter the grapes and remaining sage around the chicken and place the pan in the oven. Bake until the chicken is cooked through (the internal temperature is 165°F), 20 to 25 minutes.

5   Remove the pan from the oven and let the chicken rest for 3 minutes before serving.

Spicy Peanut Chicken with Pumpkin

1 cup peanut butter

1 tablespoon gochujang

¼ cup soy sauce

2 garlic cloves, crushed

1 red bell pepper, stem and seeds removed, cut into 1-inch squares

1 celery stalk, halved lengthwise and cut into 1-inch squares

½ small pumpkin, sliced into ½-inch-thick wedges

1 lb. chicken tenders, cut into 1-inch cubes

1 teaspoon kosher salt

Scallions, chopped, for garnish

1   Preheat the oven to 400°F. Coat a sheet pan with nonstick cooking spray.

2   Place the peanut butter, gochujang, soy sauce, and garlic in a mixing bowl and stir until thoroughly combined.

3   Add the red pepper, celery, pumpkin, and chicken to the bowl and gently toss to coat. Transfer the mixture to the sheet pan and season it with the salt.

4   Place the pan in the oven and bake until the chicken is cooked through, 15 to 20 minutes, stirring halfway through.

5   Remove the pan from the oven, garnish the dish with scallions, and serve.

Lemon Chicken & Potatoes

6 bone-in, skin-on chicken legs and thighs

1 lb. Yukon Gold potatoes, cut into wedges

¼ cup extra-virgin olive oil

3 garlic cloves, minced

1 teaspoon kosher salt

1 teaspoon black pepper

1 lemon, halved

Fresh rosemary, for garnish

1 Preheat the oven to 350°F.

2 Place the chicken and potatoes in a large mixing bowl, add the olive oil, garlic, salt, and pepper, and toss to coat.

3 Transfer the chicken and potatoes to a sheet pan, squeeze the lemon over the top, and add the halves to the pan.

4 Place the pan in the oven and bake until the chicken is cooked through (the internal temperature is 165°F) and the potatoes are tender, about 40 minutes.

5 Set the oven's broiler to high and broil until the chicken's skin is crispy, about 5 minutes.

6 Remove the pan from the oven, garnish the dish with rosemary, and serve.

Thai Chicken & Rice

6 skin-on chicken thighs

¼ cup Thai red curry paste

1½ cups long-grain rice

1 lime, sliced

1 tablespoon peanut oil

2½ cups Chicken Stock (see page 234), hot

1 garlic clove, crushed

1 tablespoon grated fresh ginger

1 lemongrass stalk (white part only), minced

1 cup green beans, trimmed and halved

¼ cup baby corn, chopped

1 tablespoon fish sauce

1 tablespoon fresh lime juice

1 scallion, trimmed and sliced thin

1 red chile pepper, stem and seeds removed, sliced thin

Roasted peanuts, chopped, for garnish

Fresh lemon balm, for garnish

1   Preheat the oven to 350°F. Place the chicken in a bowl, rub it with the curry paste, and set it aside.

2   Place the rice and lime in a sheet pan with high sides, drizzle the peanut oil over it, and stir to coat. Place the pan in the oven and toast for about 5 minutes.

3   Remove the pan from the oven and add the stock, garlic, ginger, and lemongrass. Gently stir and spread the mixture in an even layer. Arrange the chicken on top, cover the pan with aluminum foil, and return it to the oven. Bake for 25 minutes.

4   Remove the pan from the oven, remove the foil, and discard it. Move the chicken to the side and fluff the rice. Add the green beans, corn, fish sauce, and lime juice and stir to incorporate. Rearrange the chicken on top of the rice and return the pan to the oven.

5   Bake until the chicken is cooked through (the internal temperature is 165°F) and the rice is tender, 5 to 10 minutes. Top with the scallion and chile and garnish each portion with peanuts and lemon balm.

Turkey & Goat Cheese Rolls

8 turkey breast cutlets, pounded thin

1½ cups goat cheese

2 handfuls of fresh sage leaves

2 cups cherry tomatoes

2 tablespoons extra-virgin olive oil

Salt and pepper, to taste

1 Preheat the oven to 375°F. Coat a sheet pan with nonstick cooking spray.

2 Lay the turkey cutlets on a flat surface. Spread equal portions of the goat cheese down the center of each cutlet. Working with half of the sage, layer some sage on top of the goat cheese.

3 Roll up the cutlets and thread them onto two skewers. Place the skewers on the sheet pan and arrange the tomatoes around the skewers. Drizzle the olive oil over the dish and season with salt and pepper.

4 Place the pan in the oven and bake for 10 minutes.

5 While the turkey is in the oven, roughly chop most of the remaining sage leaves, making sure to keep a few of them whole.

6 Remove the pan from the oven and turn the skewers over. Sprinkle the chopped sage over the turkey rolls and scatter the whole leaves around the pan. Return the pan to the oven and bake until the turkey is cooked through (the internal temperature is 165°F), about 10 minutes.

7 Remove the pan from the oven and serve immediately.

Lemon & Pesto Chicken

8 chicken drumsticks

1 tablespoon unsalted butter, melted

2 lemons, 1 zested and juiced; 1 sliced

Salt and pepper, to taste

Pesto (see page 235)

4 plum tomatoes, halved

Fresh basil, for garnish

1   Preheat the oven to 425°F. Place the chicken on a sheet pan. Place the butter, lemon zest, and lemon juice in a small bowl and stir to combine.

2   Rub the lemon butter over the chicken and season with salt and pepper. Spoon half of the Pesto over the chicken and add the sliced lemon and tomatoes to the pan.

3   Place the pan in the oven and bake for 25 minutes.

4   Set the oven's broiler to high and broil until the chicken is cooked through (the internal temperature is 165°F) and the tomatoes are lightly charred, 5 to 10 minutes.

5   Remove the chicken from the oven, top it with the remaining Pesto, garnish with basil, and serve.

Chicken with Zucchini & Eggplant

1 large zucchini, sliced thin

1 small eggplant, sliced thin

8 chicken drumsticks

2 medium russet potatoes, peeled and cut into 1-inch cubes

2 tablespoons extra-virgin olive oil

1 teaspoon kosher salt

½ teaspoon black pepper

½ teaspoon garlic powder

½ teaspoon paprika

¼ cup pomegranate arils

1 Set the oven's broiler to high. Place the zucchini and eggplant on a sheet pan, place it in the oven, and broil until the vegetables are charred all over and cooked through, 8 to 10 minutes, turning them as necessary.

2 Remove the pan from the oven, remove the vegetables from the pan, and set them aside.

3 Preheat the oven to 425°F. Place the chicken, potatoes, olive oil, salt, pepper, garlic powder, and paprika in a mixing bowl and toss to coat. Transfer the chicken and potatoes to the sheet pan and spread them into an even layer.

4 Place the pan in the oven and roast until the chicken is almost cooked through (the internal temperature is 160°F) and the potatoes are tender, about 35 minutes, flipping the chicken over halfway through.

5 Remove the pan from the oven, add the zucchini and eggplant to the pan, and return it to the oven. Roast until the zucchini and eggplant are warmed through and the chicken is cooked through, about 5 minutes.

6 Remove the pan from the oven, sprinkle the pomegranate arils over the top, and serve.

Bacon-Wrapped Chicken with Potatoes

3 tablespoons extra-virgin olive oil

1 teaspoon Italian seasoning

1 teaspoon garlic powder

1 teaspoon kosher salt

½ teaspoon black pepper

1 tablespoon fresh lemon juice

1 tablespoon Dijon mustard

4 bone-in, skin-on chicken thighs

1 small sweet potato, cut into 1-inch cubes

1 lb. red potatoes, quartered

1 shallot, sliced

4 slices of bacon

Fresh herbs, chopped, for garnish

1 Preheat the oven to 350°F. Place the olive oil, Italian seasoning, garlic powder, salt, pepper, lemon juice, and Dijon mustard in a mixing bowl and stir to combine. Add the chicken, sweet potato, potatoes, and shallot and toss to coat.

2 Wrap a slice of bacon around each piece of chicken and place them on a sheet pan. Arrange the sweet potato, potatoes, and shallots around the chicken and place the pan in the oven. Bake until the chicken is cooked through (the internal temperature is 165°F), 40 to 45 minutes.

3 Remove the pan from the oven, garnish the dish with fresh herbs, and serve.

Roast Duck with Apples

5½ to 6 lb. whole duck

Salt and pepper, to taste

2 apples, cored and cut into wedges

1 small red onion, sliced

2 teaspoons fresh thyme

1   Preheat the oven to 425°F. Generously season the outside and inside of the duck with salt and pepper. Tie the duck's legs together with a piece of butcher's twine and place it on a sheet pan, breast side up. Place the duck in the oven and roast for 15 minutes.

2   Reduce the oven temperature to 350°F and roast the duck for another 30 minutes.

3   Remove the pan from the oven and drain any excess fat from it. Arrange the apples and onion around the duck, sprinkle the thyme over the dish, and return the pan to the oven. Roast until the duck is cooked through (the internal temperature is 165°F), about 30 minutes.

4   Remove the pan from the oven and let the duck rest for 10 minutes before serving.

Orange Chicken with Yogurt & Mint Sauce

2 bone-in, skin-on chicken legs

1½ russet potatoes, cut into wedges

1 clementine, sliced

2½ teaspoons kosher salt

1¼ teaspoons black pepper

Zest and juice of 3 clementines

4 garlic cloves, minced

¼ cup honey

½ cup orange marmalade

1 cup Greek yogurt

1 tablespoon fresh lemon juice

¼ teaspoon cumin

1 tablespoon finely chopped fresh mint

2 cups fresh spinach

1   Preheat the oven to 375°F. Line a sheet pan with parchment paper.

2   Place the chicken, potatoes, and clementine slices on the pan and season with 2 teaspoons of salt and 1 teaspoon of pepper.

3   Place the clementine zest, clementine juice, garlic, honey, and marmalade in a bowl and stir until thoroughly combined. Drizzle the sauce over the chicken, potatoes, and clementine.

4   Place the pan in the oven and roast until the chicken is cooked through (the internal temperature is 165°F) and the potatoes are tender, 30 to 35 minutes.

5   While the chicken is in the oven, place the yogurt, lemon juice, cumin, and remaining salt in a small bowl and stir to combine. Season the sauce with the remaining pepper, stir in the mint, and set the sauce aside.

6   Remove the sheet pan from the oven, stir the spinach into the dish, and serve with the dip.

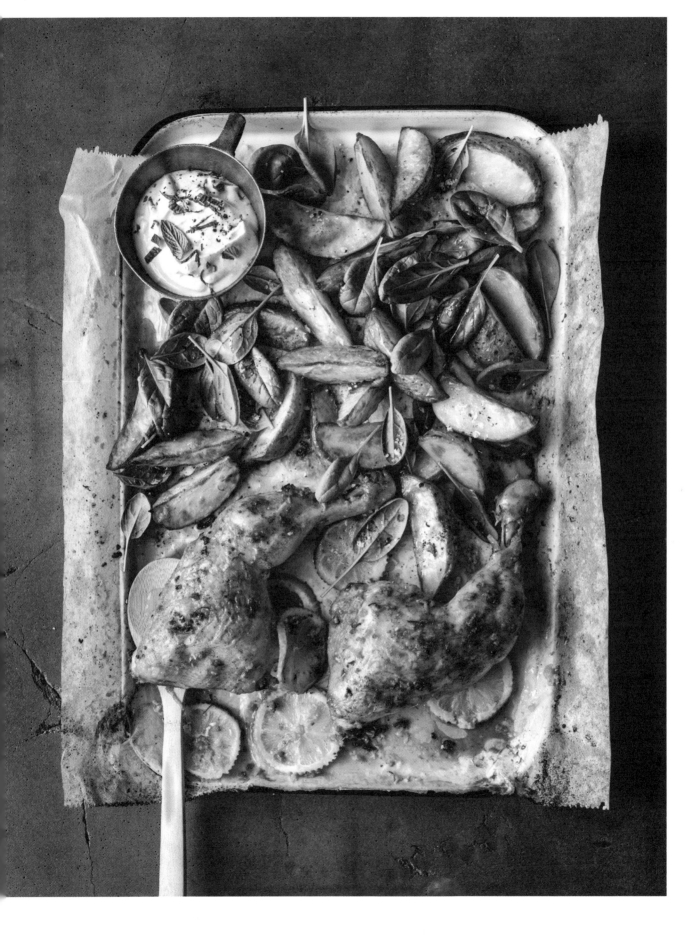

Maple Chicken with Vegetables

3 to 4 lbs. bone-in, skin-on chicken pieces

2 parsnips, scrubbed and quartered lengthwise

6 spring onions, halved lengthwise

4 tablespoons unsalted butter

¼ cup maple syrup

Cloves from 1 bulb of garlic, crushed

2 teaspoons kosher salt

1 teaspoon black pepper

½ butternut squash, peeled, seeds removed, sliced thin

½ cup pitted Sicilian olives

½ cup arugula

1 lemon, halved

1   Preheat the oven to 400°F. Arrange the chicken, parsnips, and onions on a sheet pan.

2   Place the butter, maple syrup, and garlic in a small saucepan and cook over low heat, stirring frequently, until the butter has melted.

3   Pour the mixture over the dish and season with the salt and pepper. Place the pan in the oven and bake for 30 minutes.

4   Remove the pan from the oven, add the squash, and stir to combine. Return the pan to the oven and bake until the chicken is cooked through (the internal temperature is 165°F) and the vegetables are tender, 15 to 20 minutes.

5   Remove the pan from the oven and top the dish with the olives and arugula. Squeeze the lemon over the top and serve.

Garlic & Thyme Chicken with Olives

6 bone-in, skin-on chicken legs

1 onion, sliced

½ cup pitted black olives

1 bulb of garlic, halved

½ lemon, sliced

⅓ cup Chicken Stock
(see page 234)

3 tablespoons Dijon mustard

3 tablespoons extra-virgin
olive oil

1 tablespoon fresh lemon juice

1 tablespoon maple syrup

3 garlic cloves, minced

1 tablespoon fresh thyme, plus
more for garnish

1 teaspoon kosher salt

1 teaspoon black pepper

1   Preheat the oven to 450°F. Place the chicken on a sheet pan. Arrange the onion, olives, halved bulb of garlic, and lemon slices around the chicken.

2   Place the remaining ingredients in a bowl and stir until thoroughly combined. Pour the mixture over the chicken and place the pan in the oven.

3   Roast until the chicken is cooked through (the internal temperature is 165°F), 45 to 50 minutes. Remove the pan from the oven, garnish the dish with additional thyme, and serve.

Chicken with Parsley & Shallot Sauce

1½ cups finely chopped fresh parsley

¾ cup extra-virgin olive oil

1 small shallot, minced

2 teaspoons lemon zest

3 tablespoons fresh lemon juice

¼ teaspoon kosher salt

¼ teaspoon black pepper

¼ teaspoon sugar

3½ lbs. bone-in, skin-on chicken pieces

1 fennel bulb, trimmed and cut into wedges

1 lb. red potatoes, quartered

2 peeled parsnips, halved and cut into 2-inch-long pieces

1   Place the parsley, olive oil, shallot, lemon zest, lemon juice, salt, pepper, and sugar in a mixing bowl and stir until thoroughly combined. Transfer half of the sauce to a container and set it aside. Add the chicken, fennel, potatoes, and parsnips to the sauce remaining in the bowl, toss to coat, and let the chicken and vegetables marinate in the refrigerator for 1 hour.

2   Preheat the oven to 475°F. Place the vegetables on a sheet pan in a single layer. Place the chicken, skin side up, on top of the vegetables, arranging any breasts in the center and the legs and thighs around the sides of the pan.

3   Place the pan in the oven and roast until the chicken is cooked through (the internal temperature is 165°F) and the vegetables are tender, 35 to 40 minutes, rotating the pan halfway through.

4   Remove the pan from the oven and tent it loosely with aluminum foil. Let the dish rest for 5 minutes before serving with the remaining sauce.

Yield: 4 Servings | Active Time: 35 Minutes | Total Time: 1 Hour and 15 Minutes

Chicken Kiev

½ cup unsalted butter, softened

6 garlic cloves, minced

1 cup finely chopped fresh
flat-leaf parsley, plus more for
garnish

1 teaspoon kosher salt

½ teaspoon black pepper

4 large boneless, skinless
chicken breasts

¼ cup extra-virgin olive oil

½ sourdough loaf, torn into
small pieces

Zest of 1 lemon

1 lemon, halved

1   Preheat the oven to 375°F. Line a sheet pan with parchment paper.

2   Place the butter, garlic, parsley, ½ teaspoon of salt, and ¼ teaspoon of
pepper in a bowl and stir until thoroughly combined.

3   Create a pocket in the side of each chicken breast by making an incision
with the tip of a sharp knife. Fill the pockets with the garlic mixture and
then use toothpicks to close them up. Place the chicken breasts on the
sheet pan, drizzle 2 tablespoons of olive oil over them, and season with
the remaining salt and pepper.

4   Place the bread, remaining olive oil, and the lemon zest in a mixing bowl
and toss to combine. Scatter the bread over the chicken breasts and
place the pan in the oven.

5   Roast the chicken until it is cooked through (the internal temperature is
165°F), 30 to 35 minutes. Remove the chicken from the oven and let it
rest for 5 minutes.

6   Squeeze the lemon over the dish, garnish with additional parsley,
and serve.

Jalfrezi Chicken & Vegetables

2 tablespoons extra-virgin olive oil

2 garlic cloves, minced

1 teaspoon kosher salt

1 tablespoon jalfrezi curry paste

2 tablespoons onion jam

¼ cup red wine vinegar

1 zucchini, sliced into ½-inch-thick rounds

1 cup trimmed and halved green beans

2 cups cauliflower florets

1 small jar of roasted red peppers, drained and chopped

1 small red onion, chopped

4 bone-in, skin-on chicken breasts

1   Preheat the oven to 425°F. Place the olive oil, garlic, salt, curry paste, onion jam, and vinegar in a mixing bowl and stir until thoroughly combined.

2   Place the zucchini, green beans, cauliflower, roasted red peppers, and onion on a sheet pan. Pour half of the sauce over the vegetables and toss to coat.

3   Spread the vegetables in an even layer, cut a few diagonal slits on the tops of the chicken breasts, and arrange them on top of the vegetables. Pour the remaining sauce over the chicken and place the pan in the oven.

4   Bake until the chicken is cooked through (the internal temperature is 165°F), 25 to 30 minutes. Remove the pan from the oven and let the dish rest for a few minutes before serving.

Yield: 4 Servings | Active Time: 20 Minutes | Total Time: 50 Minutes

Sherry & Sun-Dried Tomato Chicken

3 tablespoons extra-virgin olive oil

4 garlic cloves, minced

1 tablespoon smoked paprika

2 tablespoons sun-dried tomato paste

2 tablespoons sherry vinegar

1 teaspoon kosher salt

½ teaspoon black pepper

1 yellow bell pepper, stem and seeds removed, chopped

1 red bell pepper, stem and seeds removed, chopped

1 small red onion, cut into thin wedges

2 lbs. boneless, skinless chicken thighs

1   Preheat the oven to 425°F. Place the olive oil, garlic, paprika, tomato paste, vinegar, salt, and pepper in a mixing bowl and stir until thoroughly combined.

2   Place the peppers, onion, and chicken on a sheet pan in a single layer, drizzle the sauce over the top, and toss to coat.

3   Place the pan in the oven and roast until the chicken is cooked through (the internal temperature is 165°F) and the vegetables are tender, about 30 minutes.

4   Remove the pan from the oven and serve immediately.

Paprika Turkey Legs with Brussels Sprouts & Potatoes

4 bone-in, skin-on turkey legs

2 tablespoons extra-virgin olive oil

2 teaspoons kosher salt

1 teaspoon black pepper

1 teaspoon sweet paprika

½ cup Chicken Stock (see page 234)

1 lb. fingerling potatoes, quartered

1 lb. Brussels sprouts, trimmed and halved

1 tablespoon finely chopped fresh parsley

1   Preheat the oven to 400°F. Place the turkey legs in a sheet pan with high sides and drizzle half of the olive oil over them. Season with half of the salt, half of the pepper, and the paprika, add the stock, and place the pan in the oven. Bake for 20 minutes.

2   Reduce the oven's temperature to 350°F. Remove the pan from the oven and add the potatoes and Brussels sprouts. Sprinkle the parsley over the dish and return the pan to the oven.

3   Bake until the turkey legs are cooked through (the internal temperature is 165°F) and the vegetables are tender, about 40 minutes.

4   Remove the pan from the oven and serve immediately.

Chicken with Feta & Capers

1¼ lbs. waxy potatoes, cut into thick wedges

2¼ lbs. bone-in, skin-on chicken thighs

¼ cup olive oil

1 teaspoon kosher salt

½ teaspoon black pepper

2 teaspoons dried oregano

4 garlic cloves, minced

3 lemons, halved

2 tablespoons drained capers

2 small red onions, sliced thin

½ cup crumbled feta cheese

1 Preheat the oven to 350°F. Place the potatoes and chicken in a large mixing bowl, add the olive oil, salt, pepper, oregano, and garlic, and toss to coat. Transfer the potatoes and chicken to a sheet pan and arrange them in a single layer.

2 Squeeze 2 of the lemons over the dish and sprinkle the capers on top. Place the pan in the oven and roast until the chicken is browned, 45 to 50 minutes.

3 Remove the pan from the oven and sprinkle the onions and feta over the dish. Squeeze the remaining lemon over the top and add the 2 spent halves to the pan. Return the pan to the oven and roast until the chicken is cooked through (the internal temperature is 165°F) and the potatoes are tender, 5 to 10 minutes.

Chicken, Roasted Red Peppers & Eggplant

2 red bell peppers

2 eggplants, halved and sliced lengthwise

4 cups fresh spinach

2 teaspoons kosher salt

1 teaspoon black pepper

1 tablespoon white balsamic vinegar

¼ cup extra-virgin olive oil

4 bone-in, skin-on chicken thighs

8 garlic cloves

8 sprigs of fresh thyme

½ lb. cherry tomatoes

Fresh parsley, chopped, for garnish

1 Preheat the oven to 400°F. Place the bell peppers on a sheet pan, place them in the oven, and roast until they are charred all over, 15 to 20 minutes, turning them as necessary. Remove the peppers from the oven, place them in a heatproof bowl, and cover it with a kitchen towel. Let the peppers steam for 10 minutes.

2 When the peppers have cooled slightly, remove their stems, seed pods, and skins, slice the remaining flesh into long strips, and set them aside.

3 Coat a sheet pan with high sides with nonstick cooking spray. Place the eggplants in the pan, skin side up, and arrange the peppers and spinach between the slices. Season the vegetables with half of the salt and half of the pepper.

4 Place the vinegar and 1 tablespoon of olive oil in a large bowl and stir to combine. Season the mixture with the remaining salt and pepper, add the chicken, and toss to coat. Transfer the chicken to the pan, top the dish with the garlic and thyme, and drizzle the remaining olive oil over it.

5 Place the pan in the oven and bake for 30 minutes, basting the chicken halfway through.

6 Remove the pan from the oven and arrange the tomatoes on it. Return the pan to the oven and bake until the chicken is cooked through (the internal temperature is 165°F), about 15 minutes.

7 Remove the pan from the oven, garnish the dish with fresh parsley, and serve.

Yield: 4 Servings | Active Time: 25 Minutes | Total Time: 55 Minutes

Mediterranean Chicken

2 teaspoons cumin seeds

3 teaspoons dried oregano

1 teaspoon kosher salt

1 tablespoon dried thyme

1 teaspoon black pepper

½ teaspoon cinnamon

⅓ cup extra-virgin olive oil, plus more to taste

4 bone-in, skin-on chicken breasts

3 cups halved baby potatoes

1 sweet onion, cut into 1-inch-thick slices

1 lemon, cut into wedges

2 cups halved cherry tomatoes

2 tablespoons capers, drained

½ cup crumbled feta cheese

¼ cup fresh parsley

1. Preheat the oven to 400°F. Line a sheet pan with aluminum foil.

2. Place the cumin seeds, oregano, salt, thyme, pepper, cinnamon, and olive oil in a mixing bowl and stir to combine.

3. Place the chicken on the sheet pan and rub it with the seasoning mixture, reserving about 2 tablespoons.

4. Place the potatoes in the reserved seasoning mixture and toss to coat. Arrange the potatoes on the pan, add the onion and half of the lemon wedges, and roast until the chicken is cooked through (the internal temperature is 165°F) and the potatoes are tender, 30 to 40 minutes.

5. Remove the pan from the oven, sprinkle the tomatoes, capers, feta, and parsley over the dish, and serve with the remaining lemon wedges.

Chicken & Cauliflower Curry

2 tablespoons curry powder

2 teaspoons cumin

2 teaspoons coriander

1 teaspoon kosher salt

½ teaspoon black pepper

3 tablespoons extra-virgin olive oil

1 lb. bone-in, skin-on chicken pieces

2 cups cauliflower florets

1 lemon, halved

Fresh cilantro, for garnish

1   Preheat the oven to 425°F. Place the curry powder, cumin, coriander, salt, pepper, and olive oil in a mixing bowl and stir to combine.

2   Place the chicken on a sheet pan and rub it with the seasoning mixture, reserving about 1 tablespoon. Place the pan in the oven and roast it for 20 minutes.

3   Add the cauliflower to the reserved seasoning mixture and toss to coat. Remove the pan from the oven and add the cauliflower.

4   Return the pan to the oven and bake until the chicken is cooked through (the internal temperature should be 165°F) and the cauliflower is starting to brown, 20 to 25 minutes.

5   Remove the pan from the oven and let the dish rest for about 5 minutes. Squeeze the lemon over the chicken, garnish the dish with cilantro, and serve.

Chicken with Potatoes, Figs & Oranges

3 to 4 lb. whole chicken

3 small oranges, halved

2 garlic cloves

2 sprigs of fresh rosemary

1 tablespoon kosher salt

1 teaspoon black pepper

¼ cup unsalted butter, cubed

2 cups Chicken Stock
(see page 234)

2½ lbs. new potatoes

2 figs, quartered

2 shallots, peeled

2 tablespoons extra-virgin
olive oil

Aioli (see page 246), for serving

1   Preheat the oven to 375°F. Place the chicken in a sheet pan with high sides and place 2 orange halves, the garlic cloves, and the rosemary in the chicken's cavity. Season with 2 teaspoons of salt and half of the pepper, top the chicken with the butter, pour the stock into the pan, and place the pan in the oven. Bake for 1 hour.

2   Remove the pan from the oven and add the potatoes, figs, shallots, and remaining orange halves to the pan. Drizzle the olive oil over the dish and season with the remaining salt and pepper.

3   Return the pan to the oven and bake until the chicken is cooked through (the internal temperature is 165°F) and the vegetables are tender, about 30 minutes.

4   Remove the pan from the oven, tent it loosely with aluminum foil, and let the chicken rest for 10 minutes before serving alongside the Aioli.

Seafood

These dishes are where the beneficial nature of the sheet pan really becomes clear. Simple, effortless, accessible to cooks of all levels, guaranteed to taste wonderful once pulled from the oven, and the very best thing you can eat in terms of your health, seafood is a smash hit in the world of sheet pan meals, checking every single box one would want from an entree.

There's an option for every occasion in this chapter: a clambake that is sure to impress a larger crowd while keeping you out of the kitchen all night, a salmon dish featuring a brightly flavored mango salsa that was made for the early summer, and a comforting shrimp-and-noodle preparation that will scratch your itch for takeout.

Clambake

1 lb. new potatoes

1 tablespoon extra-virgin olive oil

2 teaspoons kosher salt

1 teaspoon black pepper

1 lb. mussels, rinsed well and scrubbed

1 lb. littleneck clams, rinsed well and scrubbed

2 corncobs, cut into 2-inch-long pieces

½ lb. chorizo, cut into 2-inch-long pieces

½ cup unsalted butter, cubed

2 teaspoons Old Bay Seasoning

1 lb. jumbo shrimp, shelled and deveined

1 tablespoon finely chopped fresh parsley, for garnish

Lemon wedges, for serving

1   Preheat the oven to 450°F. Line a sheet pan with aluminum foil.

2   Place the potatoes in a mixing bowl, add the olive oil, salt, and pepper, and toss to combine. Spread the potatoes on the pan in an even layer, place them in the oven, and roast until they are slightly tender, about 25 minutes.

3   Remove the pan from the oven and scatter the mussels, clams, corn, chorizo, and butter over the potatoes. Sprinkle the Old Bay Seasoning over the dish and return the pan to the oven. Roast for 15 minutes.

4   Remove the pan from the oven and add the shrimp. Stir to combine and spread the mixture into an even layer. Return the pan to the oven and roast until the majority of the mussels and clams have opened and the shrimp are pink and cooked through. Remove the pan from the oven and discard any mussels and/or clams that did not open.

5   Garnish the dish with the fresh parsley and serve with lemon wedges.

Yield: 2 Servings | Active Time: 30 Minutes | Total Time: 1 Hour

Halibut with Herbed Citrus Butter

2 lbs. halibut fillets

2 leeks, trimmed, rinsed well, and sliced

1 tablespoon extra-virgin olive oil

½ cup white wine

1 teaspoon kosher salt

½ teaspoon black pepper

½ cup unsalted butter, softened

2 tablespoons orange zest

2 tablespoons finely chopped fresh parsley

2 tablespoons finely chopped fennel fronds

1   Preheat the oven to 375°F. Lightly coat a sheet pan with nonstick cooking spray.

2   Place the halibut on the pan and surround it with the sliced leeks. Drizzle the olive oil and wine over it and season with the salt and pepper.

3   Place the pan in the oven and bake the halibut until it is cooked through and can be flaked easily with a fork, about 25 minutes.

4   While the halibut is in the oven, place the butter, orange zest, parsley, and fennel fronds in a mixing bowl and stir until thoroughly combined.

5   Remove the pan from the oven, top the halibut with dollops of the herbed butter, and serve.

Trout with Fennel

1 whole trout, gutted and cleaned

2 teaspoons kosher salt

1 teaspoon freshly ground black pepper

½ red onion, sliced thin

4 slices of lemon

¼ cup extra-virgin olive oil

2 cups snow peas, cut into ½-inch squares

½ fennel bulb, cut into 1-inch squares

1 small zucchini, cut into 1-inch cubes

1   Preheat the oven to 350°F. Coat a sheet pan with nonstick cooking spray and place the trout on it.

2   Season the inside of the trout with half of the salt and half of the pepper and then stuff it with the onion and lemon slices. Drizzle half of the olive oil over the trout, place it in the oven, and bake for 10 minutes.

3   Remove the pan from the oven and arrange the snow peas, fennel, and zucchini around the trout. Drizzle the remaining olive oil over the vegetables and season them with the remaining salt and pepper.

4   Return the pan to the oven and bake until the fish is cooked through and the vegetables are tender, 10 to 15 minutes.

5   Remove the pan from the oven and serve immediately.

Salmon with Mango & Avocado Salsa

Flesh of 2 mangoes, diced

Flesh of 1 avocado, diced

3 tablespoons fresh lime juice

1 red chile pepper, stem and seeds removed, finely diced

1 tablespoon finely chopped fresh chives

1 tablespoon kosher salt

1½ lbs. salmon fillets

1 tablespoon extra-virgin olive oil

Sesame seeds, for garnish

Lime wedges, for serving

Sour cream, for serving

Red pepper jelly, for serving

1   Preheat the oven to 400°F. Place the mangoes, avocado, lime juice, chile, chives, and 1 teaspoon of salt in a mixing bowl and stir until thoroughly combined. Set the salsa aside.

2   Coat a sheet pan with nonstick cooking spray and place the salmon in the pan. Season the salmon with the remaining salt and drizzle the olive oil over it.

3   Place the pan in the oven and bake until the salmon is cooked through, about 15 minutes.

4   Remove the pan from the oven and top the salmon with the mango salsa. Garnish with sesame seeds and serve with lime wedges, sour cream, and red pepper jelly.

Shrimp Chow Mein

2 lbs. chow mein noodles, parboiled

½ red bell pepper, cut into 1-inch-thick strips

1 cup diced broccolini

1 carrot, peeled and cut into 1-inch pieces

1 cup chopped baby corn

2 tablespoons canola oil

1 tablespoon sesame oil

¼ cup soy sauce

1½ tablespoons oyster sauce

½ lb. small shrimp, shelled and deveined

Bean sprouts, for garnish

1   Preheat the oven to 375°F. Coat a sheet pan with nonstick cooking spray.

2   Place the noodles, bell pepper, broccolini, carrot, and corn in a mixing bowl, add the canola oil, sesame oil, soy sauce, and oyster sauce, and toss to coat.

3   Transfer the mixture to the sheet pan and spread it into an even layer. Place the pan in the oven and bake for 10 minutes.

4   Remove the pan from the oven and carefully stir until the noodles and vegetables are thoroughly mixed. Top with the shrimp and return the pan to the oven.

5   Cook until the shrimp are cooked through, about 10 minutes. Remove the pan from the oven, garnish the dish with bean sprouts, and serve immediately.

Cod with Kumquats

2 lbs. cod fillets

1 teaspoon kosher salt

½ teaspoon black pepper

1 tablespoon crushed pink peppercorns

2 cups sliced kumquats

2 tablespoons extra-virgin olive oil

Fresh rosemary, for garnish

1 lime, sliced, for garnish

1   Preheat the oven to 400°F. Line a sheet pan with parchment paper.

2   Place the cod on the pan, season with the salt and black pepper, and top with the pink peppercorns. Scatter the kumquats around the cod and drizzle the olive oil over everything.

3   Place the pan in the oven and bake until the cod looks flaky and is cooked through, 12 to 15 minutes.

4   Remove the pan from the oven, garnish the dish with rosemary and the lime, and enjoy.

Rainbow Trout with Fennel, Beets & Kumquats

1 tablespoon extra-virgin olive oil

1 small rainbow trout, cleaned and butterflied

2 teaspoons kosher salt

1 teaspoon black pepper

2 slices of lemon

¼ cup thinly sliced fresh basil

4 sprigs of fresh thyme

1 large beet, peeled and sliced into thin wedges

½ fennel bulb, trimmed and sliced into thin wedges

¼ cup sliced kumquats

1 Preheat the oven to 400°F. Drizzle the olive oil over the inside of the trout and season with half of the salt and pepper. Stuff the trout with the lemon, basil, and thyme and place it on a sheet pan.

2 Scatter the beet and fennel around the trout and season with the remaining salt and pepper.

3 Place the pan in the oven and roast until the trout is cooked through and the beet and fennel are tender, about 30 minutes.

4 Remove the pan from the oven, top the dish with the kumquats, and serve.

Spicy Shrimp with Soba Noodles

½ bunch of asparagus, trimmed

½ cup shelled edamame

5 tablespoons peanut oil

Salt, to taste

½ lb. green tea soba noodles

2 tablespoons honey

⅓ cup fresh lime juice

¼ cup fish sauce

2 small red Thai chile peppers, stems and seeds removed, finely diced

12 large shrimp, shelled and deveined

Fresh mint, for garnish

Fresh Thai basil, chopped, for garnish

1   Preheat the oven to 400°F. Place the asparagus and edamame on a sheet pan, drizzle 1 tablespoon of peanut oil over them, and season with salt. Toss to coat, place the pan in the oven, and roast for 15 minutes.

2   While the vegetables are in the oven, cook the soba noodles according to the manufacturer's directions. Drain the noodles and set them aside.

3   Place the remaining peanut oil, the honey, lime juice, fish sauce, and chiles in a mixing bowl and stir until thoroughly combined.

4   Place the shrimp in a separate bowl, add half of the sauce, and toss to coat.

5   Remove the pan from the oven, arrange the shrimp on top of the vegetables, and return the pan to the oven.

6   Cook until the shrimp just turn pink and are cooked through, about 8 minutes.

7   Remove the pan from the oven, serve the shrimp and vegetables over the noodles, and garnish each portion with mint and Thai basil.

Yield: 3 Servings | Active Time: 25 Minutes | Total Time: 45 Minutes

Couscous-Crusted Snapper

1 cup plain bread crumbs

1 cup cooked and cooled couscous

1 tablespoon lemon zest

2 tablespoons extra-virgin olive oil

1 teaspoon kosher salt

½ teaspoon black pepper

3 skin-on red snapper fillets

Fresh dill, for garnish

¼ cup slivered almonds, for garnish

Lemon wedges, for serving

Sour cream, for serving

Fresh peas, cooked, for serving

1   Preheat the oven to 350°F. Coat a sheet pan with nonstick cooking spray.

2   Place the bread crumbs, couscous, lemon zest, olive oil, salt, and pepper in a mixing bowl and stir until thoroughly combined.

3   Place the red snapper on the pan, skin side down. Spread the bread crumb mixture evenly over the red snapper and gently press down on it.

4   Place the pan in the oven and bake until the red snapper is cooked through and the crust is golden brown, 15 to 20 minutes.

5   Remove the pan from the oven, garnish with dill and the slivered almonds, and serve with lemon wedges, sour cream, and peas.

Mediterranean Salmon

2 celery stalks, chopped

1 (14 oz.) can of artichoke hearts, drained and chopped

2 plum tomatoes, chopped

1 (16 oz.) jar of pepperoncini, drained and chopped

¼ small red onion, sliced

½ lemon, sliced

1 cup pitted black olives, plus more, sliced, for garnish

1 teaspoon finely chopped fresh rosemary

¼ cup extra-virgin olive oil

1 tablespoon fresh lemon juice

1 lb. salmon fillets

¼ teaspoon black pepper

1 teaspoon kosher salt

⅛ teaspoon Aleppo pepper

2 cups arugula, for serving

1   Preheat the oven to 400°F. Line a sheet pan with parchment paper.

2   Place the celery, artichoke hearts, tomatoes, pepperoncini, onion, lemon, olives, and one-third of the rosemary in the pan. Drizzle 3 tablespoons of olive oil and the lemon juice over the mixture and toss to coat.

3   Place the salmon on top of the vegetables. Sprinkle the black pepper over the entire dish. Season the salmon with the salt and Aleppo pepper, drizzle the remaining olive oil over it, and place the pan in the oven.

4   Bake until the salmon is cooked through and flakes easily at the touch of a fork, about 20 minutes. Remove the pan from the oven and sprinkle the remaining rosemary over the dish.

5   Garnish with additional black olives and serve with the arugula.

Haddock with Potatoes, Vegetables & Lemon

2 lbs. new potatoes, larger potatoes halved

2 plum tomatoes, cut into thick wedges

1 cup pitted black olives

1 zucchini, sliced

½ red onion, sliced

1½ lbs. haddock fillets, cut into 4 pieces

2 teaspoons extra-virgin olive oil

1 teaspoon kosher salt

4 slices of lemon

1 teaspoon black pepper

Fresh parsley, chopped, for garnish

1   Preheat the oven to 400°F. Coat a sheet pan with nonstick cooking spray.

2   Place the potatoes, tomatoes, olives, zucchini, and onion in the pan and stir to combine. Place the haddock on top, drizzle the olive oil over it, and season it with the salt. Place a slice of lemon on top of each piece of haddock and season the dish with the pepper.

3   Place the pan in the oven and bake until the fish is cooked through and flakes easily at the touch of a fork, about 20 minutes. Remove the pan from the oven, garnish the dish with parsley, and serve.

Kedgeree

1½ cups medium-grain rice

2 tablespoons extra-virgin olive oil

1 teaspoon curry powder

2½ cups Chicken Stock (see page 234), boiling

3 smoked haddock fillets

1 teaspoon kosher salt

2 Hard-Boiled Eggs (see page 236), quartered, for garnish

Fresh parsley, chopped, for garnish

1   Preheat the oven to 350°F. Place the rice, olive oil, and curry powder in a sheet pan with high sides. Carefully pour the stock over the mixture and gently stir to combine.

2   Arrange the haddock on top of the rice mixture, season with the salt, and cover the pan tightly with aluminum foil. Place the pan in the oven and bake for 30 minutes.

3   Carefully remove the pan from the oven, break up the haddock, and stir it into the rice.

4   Garnish the dish with the Hard-Boiled Eggs and parsley and serve.

Hake with Chermoula & Vegetables

2 garlic cloves, minced

2 tablespoons finely chopped fresh parsley

2 tablespoons finely chopped fresh cilantro

2 teaspoons sweet paprika

1 teaspoon cumin

1½ preserved lemons, chopped

5 tablespoons extra-virgin olive oil, plus more for topping

2 teaspoons kosher salt

4 beets, peeled and cut into 1-inch chunks

1 bunch of baby carrots, trimmed

1 small red onion, sliced

½ teaspoon black pepper

2 lbs. hake fillets

Fresh herbs, for garnish

2 cups yogurt, for serving

1   Preheat the oven to 400°F. Line a sheet pan with parchment paper.

2   Place the garlic, parsley, cilantro, paprika, cumin, preserved lemons, ¼ cup of olive oil, and half of the salt in a blender and puree until the mixture is smooth. Set the chermoula sauce aside.

3   Place the beets, carrots, and onion on the sheet pan, drizzle the remaining olive oil over the top, and season with the remaining salt and the pepper. Place the pan in the oven and roast the vegetables for 45 minutes.

4   Remove the pan from the oven and push the vegetables to the edges. Place the hake in the center of the pan and rub the sauce all over the fish.

5   Return the pan to the oven and bake until the hake is baked through and the vegetables are tender, 15 to 20 minutes.

6   Remove the pan from the oven and garnish the dish with fresh herbs. Place the yogurt in a bowl, drizzle some olive oil over it, and serve it alongside the hake and roasted vegetables.

Yield: 4 Servings | Active Time: 35 Minutes | Total Time: 1 Hour and 5 Minutes

Cod with Celeriac, Carrots & Potatoes

2 white potatoes, sliced thin

2 large carrots, peeled and sliced

1 small onion, peeled and sliced

1 small celeriac, peeled and sliced

¼ cup extra-virgin olive oil

1 teaspoon kosher salt, plus more to taste

1½ lbs. cod fillets, cut into 4 pieces

1 teaspoon crushed red peppercorns

Fresh rosemary, chopped, for garnish

1   Preheat the oven to 375°F. Place the vegetables on a sheet pan, drizzle half of the olive oil over them, season with half of the salt, and toss to coat.

2   Place the pan in the oven and roast until the vegetables are just tender, about 10 minutes, stirring them halfway through.

3   Remove the pan from the oven and arrange the cod on top of the vegetables. Drizzle the remaining olive oil over the dish, and season with the remaining salt and the peppercorns.

4   Return the pan to the oven and bake until the cod is just cooked through and can easily be flaked with a fork, 10 to 15 minutes.

5   Remove the pan from the oven, garnish the dish with rosemary, and serve.

Shrimp & Chicken Kebabs

½ lb. large shrimp, shelled and deveined

2 boneless, skinless chicken breasts, cut into 1-inch cubes

1 cup diced bell pepper

1 cup chopped summer squash

1 cup chopped zucchini

1 cup halved cremini mushrooms

1 cup cherry tomatoes

2 tablespoons extra-virgin olive oil

1 teaspoon kosher salt

½ teaspoon black pepper

1   Preheat the oven to 450°F. Place all of the ingredients in a large mixing bowl and toss to coat.

2   Thread the mixture onto skewers, alternating between the shrimp, chicken, and vegetables.

3   Place the skewers on a sheet pan, place it in the oven, and bake until the chicken and shrimp are cooked through and the vegetables are tender, 15 to 20 minutes.

4   Remove the pan from the oven and serve immediately.

Yield: 2 Servings | Active Time: 30 Minutes | Total Time: 45 Minutes

Sesame Salmon with Baby Bok Choy

¼ cup soy sauce

¼ cup orange juice

1 tablespoon mirin

1 teaspoon toasted sesame oil

1 teaspoon ground ginger

½ teaspoon garlic powder

3 baby bok choy, halved lengthwise

1 tablespoon extra-virgin olive oil

1 teaspoon kosher salt

¾ lb. salmon fillets, pin bones removed, cut into large pieces

Fresh cilantro, chopped, for garnish

1 scallion, chopped

Red chile pepper, finely diced, for garnish

1 Preheat the oven to 450°F. Coat a sheet pan with nonstick cooking spray.

2 Place the soy sauce, orange juice, mirin, sesame oil, ginger, and garlic powder in a mixing bowl and whisk until combined.

3 Arrange the bok choy on the pan in an even layer. Drizzle the olive oil over it and season with the salt.

4 Place the salmon on top of the bok choy, arranging it in a strip down the center. Pour the soy sauce mixture over the salmon.

5 Place the sheet pan in the oven and roast until the salmon is cooked through, 12 to 15 minutes.

6 Remove the pan from the oven, garnish the dish with cilantro, the scallion, and chile pepper, and serve.

Shrimp with Salsa Verde & Radicchio

2 radicchios, cut into large chunks

11 tablespoons extra-virgin olive oil

1 tablespoon balsamic vinegar

2 teaspoons kosher salt, plus more to taste

1 teaspoon black pepper, plus more to taste

1 lb. shrimp, shelled and deveined

2 pieces of pita bread, cut into triangles

1 cup fresh flat-leaf parsley

1 cup fresh basil

1 garlic clove, chopped

2 teaspoons capers, drained

3 tablespoons fresh lemon juice

2 tablespoons pomegranate seeds

1   Preheat the oven to 400°F. Place the radicchio on a sheet pan, drizzle half of the olive oil and half of the vinegar over it, season it with half of the salt and half of the pepper, and gently toss to coat.

2   Place the pan in the oven and roast the radicchio until it is tender and the leaves are starting to caramelize and slightly wilt, 15 to 18 minutes.

3   While the radicchio is in the oven, place the shrimp in a mixing bowl, add 1 tablespoon of olive oil and the remaining salt and pepper, and toss to combine.

4   Remove the pan from the oven, add the shrimp and pita to the pan, and return it to the oven. Bake until the shrimp has turned opaque and the pita is lightly toasted, about 5 minutes.

5   While the shrimp is in the oven, place the parsley, basil, garlic, and capers in a food processor and blitz until the mixture is finely chopped. With the food processor running, add the remaining olive oil and vinegar, and the lemon juice in a slow stream and blitz until they have emulsified. Season the salsa verde with salt and pepper and set it aside.

6   Remove the sheet pan from the oven, drizzle the salsa verde over the dish, sprinkle the pomegranate seeds on top, and serve.

Vegetables

Everyone knows that incorporating more vegetables into their diet is a game-changer in terms of health. Pairing that reality with the boost that turning in your takeout menus for a series of sheet pan dishes makes the meals in this chapter some of the best options in the entire book for those who are looking to take back their free time each evening and also keep their well-being on track.

From a delicious main built around vegetable hash and a surprisingly decadent stuffed tomato dish to a perfectly spiced mélange of cauliflower and chickpeas, here's a collection plant-forward recipes that are certain to hit the mark when something quick but nutritious is required.

Vegetable Hash

1 lb. Yukon Gold potatoes, cut into 1-inch cubes

1 tablespoon extra-virgin olive oil

1 teaspoon kosher salt, plus more to taste

1 teaspoon freshly ground black pepper, plus more to taste

1 cup quartered cremini mushrooms

2 large tomatoes, cut into 1-inch chunks

4 slices of bacon, halved

1 slice of crusty bread, cut into 1-inch cubes

4 large eggs

1 handful of kale, stems removed, leaves torn into large pieces

1 Preheat the oven to 425°F. Line a sheet pan with parchment paper.

2 Place the potatoes in a large bowl, add the olive oil, salt, and pepper, and toss to combine.

3 Place the potatoes on the sheet pan in an even layer, place them in the oven, and bake for 20 minutes.

4 Remove the sheet pan from the oven and add the mushrooms, tomatoes, bacon, and bread to the sheet pan. Stir gently to combine, return the pan to the oven, and bake until the bacon is just starting to become crispy, about 15 minutes.

5 Remove the sheet pan from the oven and crack the eggs onto the mixture. Season with salt and pepper and top with the kale.

6 Return the pan to the oven and bake until the eggs are cooked to the desired level of doneness.

7 Remove the hash from the oven and serve.

Brussels Sprouts with Red Grapes & Walnuts

1½ lbs. Brussels sprouts, trimmed and halved

1 teaspoon extra-virgin olive oil

1 teaspoon kosher salt

1 lb. red seedless grapes

½ cup walnuts

1 Preheat the oven to 375°F. Line a sheet pan with parchment paper.

2 Place the Brussels sprouts in a mixing bowl, add the olive oil and salt, and toss to combine. Transfer the mixture to the sheet pan and place it in the oven. Roast for 15 minutes.

3 Remove the pan from the oven, add the grapes and walnuts, and gently toss to combine.

4 Return the pan to the oven and roast until the Brussels sprouts are tender and the grapes are starting to collapse, 20 to 25 minutes.

5 Remove the pan from the oven and serve.

Stuffed Tomatoes

3 potatoes, peeled and cubed

¼ cup extra-virgin olive oil

2 teaspoons kosher salt

8 tomatoes

½ cup cooked Arborio rice

2 anchovy fillets, finely chopped

2 teaspoons capers

2 tablespoons finely shredded fresh basil

1 garlic clove, minced

1   Preheat the oven to 350°F. Line a sheet pan with parchment paper.

2   Place the potatoes on the sheet pan and drizzle 1 tablespoon of olive oil over them. Season with 1 teaspoon of salt and toss to combine.

3   Place the potatoes in the oven and bake for 20 minutes.

4   While the potatoes are in the oven, cut the tops off of the tomatoes and set the tops aside. Scoop the pulp out of the tomatoes and discard the excess seeds. Chop the pulp and reserve it and any juices.

5   Place the rice, tomato pulp and juices, anchovy fillets, capers, basil, garlic, and 2 tablespoons of olive oil in a mixing bowl, add the remaining salt, and stir to combine. Fill the hollowed-out tomatoes with the rice mixture and place the tops back on.

6   Remove the sheet pan from the oven, stir the potatoes, and nestle the tomatoes into the potatoes. Drizzle the remaining olive oil over the tomatoes and return the pan to the oven. Bake until the potatoes are cooked through and the tomatoes are tender, about 20 minutes.

7   Remove the pan from the oven and let the dish cool slightly before serving.

Potatoes & Carrots with Feta

4 russet potatoes, cut into wedges

1½ lbs. carrots, scrubbed and tops removed

3 garlic cloves, sliced

2 tablespoons finely chopped fresh rosemary

3 tablespoons extra-virgin olive oil

2 teaspoons kosher salt

¼ teaspoon black pepper

½ cup crumbled feta cheese

1   Preheat the oven to 400°F. Place the potatoes, carrots, garlic, and half of the rosemary in a mixing bowl, add the olive oil, and toss to combine. Place the mixture on a sheet pan in an even layer and season with the salt and pepper.

2   Place the pan in the oven and roast until the vegetables are tender, about 30 minutes, stirring halfway through.

3   Remove the pan from the oven, sprinkle the feta and remaining rosemary over the dish, and serve.

Carrots & Parsnips over Rice Pilaf

2 carrots, peeled and cut into 1-inch pieces

2 parsnips, peeled and cut into 1-inch pieces

3 tablespoons extra-virgin olive oil

1 teaspoon kosher salt

½ teaspoon black pepper

3 sprigs of fresh rosemary

Rice pilaf, for serving

1   Preheat the oven to 425°F. Place the carrots and parsnips on a sheet pan and toss with the olive oil. Season with the salt and pepper, add the fresh rosemary sprigs, and stir to combine.

2   Place the sheet pan in the oven and roast until the vegetables are tender, about 30 minutes, stirring halfway through.

3   Remove the vegetables from the oven and serve over rice pilaf.

Portobellos, Broccoli & Lentils

4 cups lentils, picked over

8 large portobello mushrooms

1 head broccoli, trimmed and chopped

2 tablespoons extra-virgin olive oil

1 teaspoon kosher salt

½ teaspoon black pepper

1 tablespoon finely chopped fresh sage

2 garlic cloves, sliced thin

¾ cup dry white wine

⅓ cup chopped walnuts

1 cup crumbled feta cheese

2 cups baby arugula

1   Bring water to a boil in a large pot. Add the lentils and cook until they are tender but before they start falling apart, 20 to 25 minutes. Drain the lentils and set them aside.

2   Preheat the oven to 400°F. Coat a sheet pan with nonstick cooking spray.

3   Place the mushrooms, stem side up, and broccoli on the sheet pan. Drizzle the olive oil over the vegetables, season with the salt and pepper, and stir to coat. Add the sage, garlic, and wine and cover the pan tightly with aluminum foil.

4   Place the pan in the oven and bake for 20 minutes.

5   Remove the sheet pan from the oven, remove the foil, and discard it. Add the lentils and walnuts, stir to incorporate, and return the pan to the oven. Cook for another 10 minutes.

6   Remove the pan from the oven, top the dish with the feta and arugula, and serve.

Curried Cauliflower & Chickpeas

¼ cup curry paste

1 head of cauliflower, trimmed and cut into large florets

1 (14 oz.) can of chickpeas, drained and rinsed

1 small red onion, sliced

1 teaspoon kosher salt

½ teaspoon black pepper

1 lemon, cut into wedges

2 cups cherry tomatoes

½ cup Greek yogurt, for garnish

Fresh cilantro, for garnish

1   Preheat the oven to 400°F. Coat a sheet pan with nonstick cooking spray.

2   Place the curry paste in a large bowl, add the cauliflower, chickpeas, and onion, and toss to combine. Transfer the mixture to the pan, season with the salt and pepper, and add the lemon wedges and tomatoes.

3   Place the pan in the oven and roast until the cauliflower is tender and starting to char, about 40 minutes.

4   Remove the pan from the oven, garnish with the yogurt and cilantro, and serve.

Yield: 4 Servings | Active Time: 20 Minutes | Total Time: 1 Hour

Provençal Brussels Sprouts & Pumpkin

1 lb. Brussels sprouts, trimmed and halved

2 cups cubed pumpkin

2 tablespoons extra-virgin olive oil

1 tablespoon balsamic vinegar

2 teaspoons herbes de Provençe

½ teaspoon kosher salt

½ teaspoon black pepper

Rice, cooked, for serving

1 Preheat the oven to 425°F. Place all of the ingredients, except for the rice, in a mixing bowl and toss to combine.

2 Place the vegetables on a sheet pan in an even layer and place them in the oven.

3 Roast until the vegetables are tender and slightly caramelized, about 30 to 40 minutes, stirring halfway through.

4 Remove the pan from the oven and serve over rice.

Stuffed Eggplants

2 large eggplants, halved lengthwise

¼ cup extra-virgin olive oil

1 onion, finely diced

2 garlic cloves, minced

1 teaspoon red pepper flakes

½ cup diced tomatoes

1 lb. ground beef

1 teaspoon kosher salt

½ teaspoon black pepper

Fresh basil, finely chopped, for garnish

1   Preheat the oven to 400°F. Scoop the flesh of each eggplant out to create a hollow center. Finely dice the flesh, place it in a large mixing bowl, and set it aside.

2   Place the eggplants on a sheet pan, cut side up, and drizzle 2 tablespoons of olive oil over them. Place the eggplants in the oven and roast until they are tender, about 20 minutes.

3   While the eggplants are in the oven, place the remaining olive oil in a large skillet and warm it over medium-high heat. Add the onion, garlic, and red pepper flakes and cook, stirring frequently, until the onion starts to soften, about 5 minutes.

4   Add the chopped eggplant, tomatoes, and beef to the pan, season with the salt and pepper, and cook, breaking up the beef with a wooden spoon, until it is browned all over, about 6 minutes. Remove the pan from heat.

5   Remove the sheet pan from the oven and fill the cavities in the eggplants with the beef mixture. Place the stuffed eggplants in the oven and bake until the edges start to brown, 5 to 10 minutes.

6   Remove the stuffed eggplants from the oven, garnish with fresh basil, and serve.

Yield: 2 to 4 Servings | Active Time: 30 Minutes | Total Time: 1 Hour and 10 Minutes

Sweet Potato & Broccoli Salad

1 sweet potato, cut into batons

2 tablespoons extra-virgin olive oil

1 teaspoon kosher salt

½ teaspoon black pepper

2 cups broccoli florets

1 cup shredded purple cabbage

4 slices of bacon

½ mango, sliced thin

¼ cup Green Goddess Dressing (see page 239), for serving

1   Preheat the oven to 400°F. Line a sheet pan with parchment paper.

2   Place the sweet potato on the sheet pan, drizzle the olive oil over it, and season with the salt and pepper. Toss to coat and arrange the sweet potato in an even single layer. Place the pan in the oven and roast for 15 minutes.

3   Remove the pan from the oven, add the broccoli and cabbage, and toss gently to combine. Lay the slices of bacon over the mixture and return the pan to the oven. Roast until the bacon is crispy and the potato and broccoli are tender, 20 to 25 minutes.

4   Remove the pan from the oven, remove the pieces of bacon, and set them aside to cool. Transfer the vegetable mixture to a mixing bowl and add the mango.

5   When the bacon has cooled slightly, chop it and add it to the mixing bowl. Gently toss to combine and serve with the Green Goddess Dressing.

Carrot & Okra Salad

1½ lbs. baby carrots, trimmed

1 tablespoon extra-virgin olive oil

1 tablespoon tajín

1 cup trimmed and halved okra

1 cup grated zucchini

½ cup red sorrel lettuce

½ cup lamb's lettuce

1 cup puffed millet, toasted

½ cup Lemon & Tahini Dressing (see page 245)

Toasted almonds, chopped, for garnish

1 Preheat the oven to 400°F. Place the carrots on a sheet pan, drizzle the olive oil over them, season with half of the tajín, and toss to coat. Place the pan in the oven and roast the carrots for 15 minutes.

2 Remove the sheet pan from the oven and add the okra and remaining tajín. Gently toss to combine and return the pan to the oven. Roast until the carrots and okra are tender, about 10 minutes.

3 Remove the pan from the oven and transfer the mixture to a bowl. Add the zucchini, lettuces, millet, and dressing and toss to combine.

4 Garnish the salad with the almonds and serve.

Yield: 4 Servings | Active Time: 25 Minutes | Total Time: 1 Hour

Chinese Eggplants & Garden Vegetables

4 Chinese eggplants, halved lengthwise and cut into wedges

6 Roma tomatoes, stems removed, halved

1 yellow bell pepper, stem and seeds removed, sliced

½ zucchini, cut into thick slices

1 garlic clove, sliced

1 tablespoon extra-virgin olive oil

1 teaspoon kosher salt

1 tablespoon finely chopped fresh oregano

½ cup crumbled Grana Padano cheese

1 Preheat the oven to 400°F. Line a sheet pan with parchment paper.

2 Place all of the ingredients, except for half of the oregano and the cheese, in a mixing bowl and toss to combine.

3 Place the mixture on the sheet pan and place it in the oven. Roast until the vegetables are tender and starting to char, 30 to 40 minutes, stirring halfway through.

4 Remove the pan from the oven, top the dish with the remaining oregano and the cheese, and serve.

Tempeh with Broccoli & Lentils

1 cup green lentils

5 tablespoons extra-virgin olive oil

2 tablespoons maple syrup

4 teaspoons apple cider vinegar

½ lb. tempeh, cubed

3 cups broccoli florets

1 tablespoon coconut oil, melted

1 teaspoon kosher salt, plus more to taste

½ teaspoon black pepper, plus more to taste

¼ cup chopped hazelnuts

½ cup almonds

½ lemon, sliced thin

Fresh parsley, chopped, for garnish

Lemon zest, for garnish

1   Preheat the oven to 400°F. Bring water to a boil in a medium pot. Add the lentils and cook until they are tender, about 20 minutes. Drain the lentils and set them aside.

2   Place the olive oil, syrup, and vinegar in a mixing bowl and stir to combine. Add the tempeh and toss to coat.

3   Place the tempeh and broccoli on a sheet pan, drizzle the coconut oil over the top, and season with the salt and pepper. Toss to coat, place the pan in the oven, and bake for 20 minutes.

4   Remove the pan from the oven, add the lentils, hazelnuts, almonds, and lemon slices to the pan, season with salt and pepper, and stir to coat. Return the pan to the oven and bake until the broccoli is tender and the nuts are toasted, 5 to 10 minutes.

5   Remove the pan from the oven, garnish the dish with parsley and lemon zest, and serve.

Baked Shells with Pumpkin & Mozzarella

1½ teaspoons kosher salt, plus more to taste

1 lb. shell pasta

1½ lbs. pumpkin, diced into ½-inch cubes

¼ teaspoon white pepper

¼ teaspoon freshly grated nutmeg

3 tablespoons extra-virgin olive oil

¼ teaspoon black pepper

1 cup ricotta cheese

1 cup mozzarella cheese, torn

Fresh rosemary, chopped, for garnish

1. Preheat the oven to 425°F. Bring water to a boil in a large pot. Add salt and the pasta and cook until the pasta is just al dente, 5 to 6 minutes. Drain the pasta and set it aside.

2. Place the pumpkin in a mixing bowl, season it with the salt, white pepper, and nutmeg, add half of the olive oil, the black pepper, and the pasta, and toss to coat. Transfer the mixture to a sheet pan, place it in the oven, and bake until the pumpkin is tender, 15 to 20 minutes.

3. Remove the pan from the oven, drizzle the remaining olive oil over it, and toss to coat. Top the dish with the ricotta and mozzarella, garnish with rosemary, and serve.

Lentils with Tomatoes & Tortilla Chips

1 cup red lentils, picked over

1 teaspoon kosher salt

1 teaspoon cumin

⅛ teaspoon cayenne pepper

2 garlic cloves, minced

1 cup corn

1 (14 oz.) can of crushed tomatoes

1 cup shredded cheddar cheese

Fresh cilantro, chopped, for garnish

Fresh basil, chopped, for garnish

Tortilla chips, for serving

Sour cream, for serving

1   Preheat the oven to 350°F. Line a sheet pan with parchment paper.

2   Place the lentils in a medium saucepan and cover them with cold water. Place over medium-high heat and bring to a boil. Cook until the lentils are just starting to become tender, about 2 minutes. Drain the lentils and rinse them under cold water to halt the cooking process.

3   Shake out any excess water and then transfer the lentils to the sheet pan.

4   Add the salt, cumin, cayenne, garlic, corn, and tomatoes and gently stir to combine. Top the dish with the cheese and place the pan in the oven. Bake until the lentils are tender and the cheese has melted, 8 to 12 minutes.

5   Remove the pan from the oven, garnish the dish with cilantro and basil, and serve with tortilla chips and sour cream.

Coconut Curry Rice with Cashews & Snow Peas

4 cups leftover white rice

1 (14 oz.) can of coconut milk

1 tablespoon curry powder

½ teaspoon turmeric powder

1 teaspoon cumin

1 teaspoon kosher salt

¼ teaspoon black pepper

1 cup snow peas

1 teaspoon extra-virgin olive oil

1 small red bell pepper, stem and seeds removed, julienned

2 tablespoons cashews

Lime wedges, for serving

1   Preheat the oven to 400°F. Coat a sheet pan with nonstick cooking spray.

2   Place the rice, coconut milk, curry, turmeric, cumin, salt, and black pepper in a bowl and stir until well combined. Transfer the rice mixture to the sheet pan and spread it in an even layer.

3   Place the snow peas in a bowl, drizzle the olive oil over them, and toss to coat. Arrange the snow peas, bell pepper, and cashews on top of the rice mixture and place the pan in the oven.

4   Bake until the rice has absorbed the liquid and the vegetables are tender, 10 to 12 minutes. Remove the pan from the oven and serve with lime wedges.

Eggplant Gratin

¼ cup extra-virgin olive oil

2 small eggplants, halved lengthwise

½ teaspoon kosher salt, plus more to taste

¼ teaspoon black pepper, plus more to taste

1 cup crushed tomatoes

1 garlic clove, minced

½ teaspoon dried oregano

½ lb. fresh mozzarella cheese, diced

½ lb. grape tomatoes, sliced

Fresh basil, for garnish

1   Preheat the oven to 425°F and coat a sheet pan with 1 tablespoon of olive oil.

2   Place 2 tablespoons of olive oil in a large skillet and warm it over medium-high heat. Season the eggplants with the salt and pepper and place them in the skillet, cut side down. Sear until the eggplants are golden brown, 3 to 4 minutes.

3   Place the crushed tomatoes, garlic, and oregano in a mixing bowl, season with salt and pepper, and stir to combine.

4   Place the eggplants on the sheet pan, cut side up, and spread the tomato sauce over them. Top with the mozzarella and grape tomatoes, season with salt and pepper, and drizzle the remaining olive oil over them.

5   Place the pan in the oven and bake until the eggplants have collapsed and the mozzarella is melted, 15 to 20 minutes.

6   Remove the eggplants from the oven, garnish with basil, and enjoy.

Quinoa-Crusted Zucchini

1 cup quinoa

1½ teaspoons kosher salt

1¾ cups water

4 small zucchini, halved lengthwise

2 tablespoons extra-virgin olive oil

½ teaspoon black pepper

2 spring onions, chopped

2 garlic cloves, minced

1 small eggplant, finely diced

1 tablespoon red wine vinegar

1 tablespoon finely chopped fresh rosemary

5 sun-dried tomatoes in olive oil, drained and chopped

3 tablespoons pine nuts

1   Place the quinoa, ½ teaspoon of salt, and the water in a medium saucepan and bring to a boil. Reduce the heat so that the quinoa simmers, cover the pan, and cook until the quinoa is tender and has absorbed all of the water, 14 to 16 minutes. Remove the pan from heat and let the quinoa sit, covered, for 10 minutes. Fluff the quinoa with a fork and set it aside.

2   Preheat the oven to 350°F. Line a sheet pan with parchment paper.

3   Using a spoon, scoop out some of the flesh from the center of the zucchini. Finely chop the removed flesh and place it in a mixing bowl.

4   Place the hollowed-out zucchini on the sheet pan in a single layer. Drizzle half of the olive oil over the zucchini and season with ½ teaspoon of salt and ¼ teaspoon of pepper. Toss to coat, place the zucchini in the oven, and roast until it is just tender, 12 to 15 minutes.

5   While the zucchini is roasting in the oven, place the remaining olive oil in a medium skillet and warm it over medium-high heat. Add the spring onions and garlic and cook, stirring continually, for 1 minute.

6   Add the eggplant and chopped zucchini to the pan, season with the remaining salt and pepper, and cook, stirring occasionally, until the eggplant and zucchini have softened, 8 to 10 minutes.

7   Stir in the vinegar and half of the rosemary and cook for 1 minute. Remove the pan from heat and stir in the cooked quinoa and sun-dried tomatoes.

8   Remove the zucchini from the oven and spoon the eggplant mixture into the zucchini's hollowed-out cavities. Sprinkle the pine nuts and remaining rosemary over the top and return the pan to the oven.

9   Roast until the quinoa crust is browned and the zucchini is completely tender, 10 to 15 minutes.

Pasta Bake with Vegetable Ragout

1 lb. ground beef

2 tablespoons extra-virgin olive oil, plus more as needed

1 small onion, finely diced

1 small carrot, peeled and finely diced

2 celery stalks, peeled and finely diced

2 garlic cloves, minced

1¼ teaspoons kosher salt, plus more to taste

1 cup red wine

1 (14 oz.) can of crushed tomatoes

1 cup Beef Stock (see page 237)

½ teaspoon dried oregano

½ teaspoon dried basil

½ teaspoon black pepper, plus more to taste

1 lb. rigatoni

Béchamel Sauce (see page 238)

1 cup shredded mozzarella cheese

Fresh basil, for garnish

1   Place the beef in a large skillet and cook over medium heat, breaking it up with a wooden spoon, until it is browned all over, 6 to 8 minutes. Drain excess grease from the pan and set the browned beef aside.

2   Place the olive oil in the pan and warm it over medium heat. Add the onion, carrot, celery, garlic, and ½ teaspoon of salt and cook, stirring frequently, until the vegetables are tender, about 8 minutes.

3   Stir in the wine and browned beef and cook until the liquid has almost completely evaporated. Stir in the tomatoes, stock, dried herbs, ½ teaspoon of salt, and ¼ teaspoon of pepper. Bring to a rapid simmer, reduce the heat so that the mixture gently simmers, and cook until it has thickened, 40 to 45 minutes, stirring occasionally.

4   While the beef-and-vegetable mixture is simmering, bring water to a boil in a large pot. Add salt and the rigatoni and cook until it is just al dente, about 4 minutes. Drain the pasta and place it in a sheet pan with high sides.

5   Add the beef-and-vegetable mixture to the sheet pan and stir to combine. Top the dish with the Béchamel Sauce and mozzarella and place it in the oven.

6   Bake until the top is golden brown and the sauce is bubbling, 40 to 45 minutes. Remove the pan from the oven and let the dish rest for 5 minutes. Garnish with basil and serve.

Acorn Squash with Polenta & Sage

For the Polenta

1 cup polenta

4 cups water

1 tablespoon extra-virgin olive oil

1 teaspoon kosher salt

½ teaspoon freshly ground black pepper

1 tablespoon unsalted butter

For the Squash

1 small acorn squash, peeled, seeded, and cut into thin wedges and bite-size cubes

1 large handful of fresh sage leaves

½ lb. cherry tomatoes

3 tablespoons extra-virgin olive oil

Salt and pepper, to taste

¾ cup fresh Parmesan cheese

1   To begin preparations for the polenta, preheat the oven to 350°F. Place the polenta, water, olive oil, salt, and pepper in a sheet pan with high sides and stir to combine.

2   Place the pan in the oven and bake the polenta for 45 minutes.

3   Remove the pan from the oven and stir in the butter. Return the pan to the oven and bake the polenta for 15 minutes.

4   Remove the polenta from the oven, stir it, and return it to the oven. Bake until it is set and firm, about 10 minutes.

5   Remove the pan from the oven and let the polenta cool to room temperature. Cover the pan with aluminum foil and chill the polenta in the refrigerator for 1 hour.

6   Turn the polenta onto a cutting board, cut it into large, bite-size cubes, and set it aside.

7   To begin preparations for the squash, preheat the oven to 375°F. Place the squash, sage, tomatoes, polenta cubes, and olive oil in a bowl, season with salt and pepper, and gently stir to combine. Place the mixture on a sheet pan, top it with half of the Parmesan, and place it in the oven.

8   Roast until the squash is extremely tender, 30 to 40 minutes. Remove the pan from the oven, top the dish with the remaining Parmesan, and serve.

Yield: 2 Servings | Active Time: 25 Minutes | Total Time: 1 Hour and 15 Minutes

Spaghetti Squash with Spinach & Cheese

1 spaghetti squash

2 tablespoons extra-virgin olive oil

1 cup baby spinach

¼ cup heavy cream

1½ cups shredded mozzarella cheese

1 teaspoon kosher salt

¼ teaspoon black pepper, plus more to taste

Edible flowers, for garnish

1   Preheat the oven to 350°F. Cut the squash in half lengthwise, remove the seeds, and brush each cut side with ½ tablespoon of olive oil. Place the squash on a sheet pan, cut side down, place it in the oven, and roast for 40 minutes.

2   Remove the pan from the oven and increase the oven's temperature to 400°F. Let the squash cool slightly, turn it over, and scoop out the flesh. Transfer the flesh to a mixing bowl and set the hollowed-out halves to the side.

3   Add the spinach, heavy cream, and half of the mozzarella to the bowl, season it with the salt and pepper, and stir to combine. Divide the mixture between the hollowed-out squash halves and top it with the remaining mozzarella. Season with pepper and place the pan in the oven.

4   Roast until the cheese has melted, about 10 minutes. Remove the pan from the oven, garnish the dish with edible flowers, and serve.

Vegetables with Tapenade & Pistachio Gremolata

1 small green cabbage, cut into 1-inch-thick rounds

¼ cup extra-virgin olive oil

1 teaspoon kosher salt

1 small pumpkin, peeled, seeded, and cut into 1-inch-thick wedges

3 tablespoons grated fresh turmeric

1 teaspoon Aleppo pepper

Tapenade (see page 243)

½ lb. yellow baby beets, boiled and halved

½ lb. red baby beets, boiled and halved

½ cup olives

Pistachio Gremolata (see page 242), for garnish

Fresh cilantro, chopped, for garnish

1. Preheat the oven to 400°F. Place the cabbage on a sheet pan, brush it with 1 tablespoon of olive oil, season it with half of the salt, and place it in the oven. Roast for 20 minutes.

2. Remove the pan from the oven and arrange the pumpkin on the pan in a single layer. Brush the pumpkin with 1 tablespoon of olive oil, season it with the remaining salt, and return the pan to the oven. Roast until the pumpkin is tender, 20 to 25 minutes.

3. Remove the pan from the oven. Place the remaining olive oil, the turmeric, and Aleppo pepper in a bowl and stir to combine. Spread the Tapenade over the roasted vegetables, add the beets, olives, and olive oil dressing, and toss to coat.

4. Garnish the dish with the gremolata and fresh cilantro and serve.

Yield: 4 Servings | Active Time: 20 Minutes | Total Time: 35 Minutes

Chiles, Cherry Tomatoes & Chickpeas

1½ teaspoons brown mustard seeds

2 teaspoons cumin seeds

½ teaspoon red pepper flakes

2 teaspoons turmeric

⅓ cup extra-virgin olive oil

¼ cup curry leaves, plus more to taste

6 long red chile peppers, seeds and stems removed, halved lengthwise

1 (14 oz.) can of chickpeas, drained, rinsed, and patted dry

1 lb. cherry tomatoes

1 teaspoon kosher salt

½ teaspoon black pepper

2 cups Greek yogurt, for serving

1 Preheat the oven to 400°F. Line a sheet pan with parchment paper.

2 Place the mustard seeds, cumin seeds, red pepper flakes, turmeric, olive oil, and curry leaves in a large bowl and stir to combine. Add the chiles, chickpeas, and tomatoes, season with the salt and pepper, and toss gently to coat.

3 Transfer the mixture to the pan and top with additional curry leaves. Place the pan in the oven and roast until the chiles are tender and the tomatoes have collapsed, 15 to 20 minutes, stirring occasionally.

4 Remove the pan from the oven and serve with the yogurt.

Yield: 4 Servings | Active Time: 30 Minutes | Total Time: 1 Hour and 10 Minutes

Duck-Fat Roasted Vegetables

5 small beets, peeled and halved

½ cup trimmed and halved Brussels sprouts

½ lb. cipollini onions

2 parsnips, peeled and halved lengthwise

¼ cup rendered duck fat, melted

1 garlic bulb, top ½ inch removed

1 teaspoon kosher salt

½ teaspoon black pepper

1 teaspoon fresh thyme, plus more for garnish

Fresh rosemary, finely chopped, for garnish

1 Preheat the oven to 400°F. Line the bottom of a sheet pan with parchment paper.

2 Place the beets, Brussels sprouts, onions, and parsnips in a bowl, add three-quarters of the duck fat, and toss to coat. Transfer the vegetables to the sheet pan.

3 Drizzle the remaining duck fat over the garlic and add it to the pan. Season the dish with the salt, pepper, and thyme, place it in the oven, and roast until the vegetables are tender, about 40 minutes.

4 Remove the pan from the oven, garnish the dish with rosemary and additional thyme, and serve.

Sweet Potatoes, Peppers & Feta

2 sweet potatoes, peeled and diced

2 zucchini, sliced

1 red bell pepper, stem and seeds removed, diced

½ lb. cherry tomatoes, halved

1 red onion, diced

3 tablespoons extra-virgin olive oil

3 garlic cloves, minced

1 teaspoon chili powder

½ teaspoon cumin

½ teaspoon smoked paprika

1 teaspoon kosher salt, plus more to taste

½ teaspoon black pepper, plus more to taste

½ lb. feta cheese

Fresh cilantro, chopped, for garnish

1   Preheat the oven to 425°F. Coat a sheet pan with high sides with nonstick cooking spray.

2   Place the sweet potatoes, zucchini, bell pepper, tomatoes, and onion in the pan in a single layer. Add the olive oil, garlic, chili powder, cumin, and paprika, season with the salt and pepper, and gently toss to combine.

3   Place the pan in the oven and bake until the sweet potatoes are tender, about 20 minutes, stirring halfway through.

4   Remove the pan from the oven and set the feta on top of the vegetable mixture. Return the pan to the oven.

5   Bake until the feta is warmed through, about 5 minutes. Remove the pan from the oven and break up the feta with a fork. Toss to combine, garnish the dish with cilantro, and serve immediately.

Yield: 2 to 4 Servings | Active Time: 25 Minutes | Total Time: 1 Hour and 15 Minutes

Rigatoni with Mushrooms & Tomatoes

1 teaspoon kosher salt, plus more to taste

½ lb. rigatoni

½ cup unsalted butter, softened

5 garlic cloves, crushed

¾ lb. baby bella mushrooms

¾ lb. white mushrooms

1 cup halved red grape tomatoes

1 cup halved yellow grape tomatoes

½ cup pine nuts

½ teaspoon black pepper

1 tablespoon fresh lemon juice

Fresh parsley, chopped, for garnish

1 Preheat the oven to 400°F. Bring water to a boil in a large pot. Add salt and the pasta and cook until the pasta is just about al dente, 4 to 6 minutes. Drain the pasta and set it aside.

2 Place the butter and garlic in a mixing bowl and stir until combined. Add the mushrooms and stir to coat.

3 Place the tomatoes, pine nuts, and mushrooms on a sheet pan, season with the salt and pepper, and sprinkle the lemon juice over the top.

4 Place the pan in the oven and bake until the tomatoes start to collapse and the mushrooms start to brown, 20 to 25 minutes.

5 Remove the pan from the oven, add the pasta, and stir to combine. Return the pan to the oven and cook until the pasta is al dente, 10 to 15 minutes.

6 Remove the pan from the oven, garnish with fresh parsley, and serve.

Vegetable Paella

1 cup Arborio rice

1 kohlrabi, peeled and cubed

2½ cups Vegetable Stock (see page 233)

1 teaspoon saffron threads

1 bay leaf

1 teaspoon paprika

3 garlic cloves, minced

1 teaspoon kosher salt

½ teaspoon black pepper

1 cup fire-roasted diced tomatoes, drained

½ red bell pepper, chopped

1 small carrot, peeled and diced

1 tablespoon extra-virgin olive oil

Scallions, sliced, for garnish

Sour cream, for serving

1   Preheat the oven to 350°F. Coat a sheet pan with high sides with nonstick cooking spray.

2   Arrange the rice and kohlrabi in the pan in an even layer, place it in the oven, and roast for 5 minutes.

3   Place the stock, saffron, bay leaf, paprika, garlic, salt, and pepper in a mixing bowl and stir to combine. Remove the pan from the oven, pour the mixture over the toasted rice and kohlrabi, and gently stir. Cover the pan loosely with aluminum foil and return the pan to the oven. Bake for 15 minutes.

4   Remove the pan from the oven, remove the foil from the pan, and discard it. Stir in the tomatoes, bell pepper, and carrot, spread the mixture into an even layer, and drizzle the olive oil over the top.

5   Return the pan to the oven and bake until the rice and vegetables are tender, and the rice has absorbed all of the liquid.

6   Remove the pan from the oven, garnish the dish with scallions, and serve with sour cream.

Vegetable & Polenta Quiche

4 cups water

1 cup instant polenta

1½ teaspoons kosher salt

1 cup whole milk

2 tablespoons unsalted butter

½ cup grated mozzarella cheese

4 large eggs

¼ cup Pesto (see page 235)

1 cup peas

1 cup diced zucchini

2 cups halved cherry tomatoes

½ cup grated Parmesan cheese

½ teaspoon black pepper

1   Preheat the oven to 400°F. Line a sheet pan with parchment paper.

2   Place the water in a medium saucepan and bring to a boil. While stirring continually, add the polenta in a slow stream. Add ½ teaspoon of salt and cook, stirring continually, until the polenta bubbles and starts to pull away from the side of the pan, about 3 minutes. Stir in the milk, butter, and mozzarella and cook until the polenta is smooth and creamy.

3   Spread the polenta over the sheet pan and use a rubber spatula to shape the edges of the polenta slightly higher than the center.

4   Place the eggs and Pesto in a mixing bowl and whisk to combine. Add the peas and zucchini and stir to incorporate. Pour the egg mixture over the polenta base and sprinkle the tomatoes and Parmesan over the top of the eggs. Season with the pepper and remaining salt.

5   Place the pan in the oven and bake until the eggs are set, about 20 minutes.

6   Remove the quiche from the oven and let it rest for 5 minutes before slicing and serving.

Baked Tofu & Vegetable Curry

3 tablespoons yellow curry paste

1½ cups coconut milk

1½ lbs. pumpkin, seeds removed, cut into ¾-inch wedges

6 small carrots, peeled and trimmed

1 bunch of broccolini, trimmed and halved lengthwise

½ cup baby corn

6 oz. extra-firm tofu, drained and cubed

1 teaspoon kosher salt

1 cup brown rice

Juice of ½ lime

Fresh cilantro, chopped, for garnish

Lime wedges, for serving

1   Preheat the oven to 400°F. Place the curry paste and coconut milk in a bowl and whisk until combined.

2   Arrange the pumpkin, carrots, broccolini, baby corn, and tofu in a sheet pan with high sides, pour the coconut milk mixture into the pan, and season with the salt. Place the pan in the oven and bake until the vegetables are tender, about 35 minutes.

3   While the pan is in the oven, prepare the brown rice according to the manufacturer's instructions.

4   Remove the pan from the oven and squeeze the lime half over the dish. Serve it over the brown rice, garnish each portion with cilantro, and serve with lime wedges.

Cauliflower & Chickpea Pilaf

¼ cup harissa

1 garlic clove, minced

1 tablespoon extra-virgin olive oil

1 head of cauliflower, trimmed and cut into florets

2¼ cups Vegetable Stock (see page 233)

1 teaspoon saffron threads

1 cup basmati rice

1 (14 oz.) can of chickpeas, drained and rinsed

¼ cup raisins

¼ cup sliced almonds

Juice of ½ lemon

1 teaspoon kosher salt

½ cup pomegranate arils

½ red onion, sliced thin

Fresh parsley, chopped, for garnish

Lemon wedges, for serving

1   Preheat the oven to 400°F. Place 2 tablespoons of harissa, the garlic, olive oil, and cauliflower in a mixing bowl and toss to coat. Transfer the cauliflower to a sheet pan with high sides, place it in the oven, and roast for 15 minutes.

2   While the cauliflower is in the oven, place the stock, remaining harissa, and the saffron in a medium saucepan and bring to a simmer. Reduce the heat to low and keep the mixture warm.

3   Remove the sheet pan from the oven, add the rice, chickpeas, raisins, and half of the almonds, and gently stir to combine. Carefully pour in the warm stock and lemon juice, season with the salt, and cover the pan with aluminum foil.

4   Return the pan to the oven and cook until the rice has absorbed all of the liquid, about 20 minutes.

5   Remove the pan from the oven and sprinkle the pomegranate arils, onion, and remaining almonds over the top. Garnish with parsley and serve with lemon wedges.

Yield: 6 Servings | Active Time: 35 Minutes | Total Time: 1 Hour and 30 Minutes

Beets Stuffed with Lentils & Quince

12 small beets

1 tablespoon extra-virgin olive oil

2 teaspoons kosher salt

1 teaspoon black pepper

3 cups Vegetable Stock (see page 233)

1 cup yellow lentils

3 tablespoons unsalted butter

1 shallot, minced

1 quince, peeled, cored, and finely diced

1 teaspoon sugar

1 teaspoon curry powder

½ teaspoon cumin

¼ cup apple cider

Fresh thyme, for garnish

1   Preheat the oven to 375°F. Line a sheet pan with parchment paper. Trim the tops and bottoms from the beets so that they can stand upright in the pan.

2   Place the beets on the pan, drizzle the olive oil over them, and season with half of the salt and half of the pepper. Place the beets in the oven and roast until the beets are tender enough to remove their cores with a knife, about 25 minutes.

3   Remove the pan from the oven, cut out the insides of the beets, and reserve for another recipe.

4   Place the stock in a medium saucepan and bring to a boil. Add the lentils, return to a boil, and then reduce the heat so that the lentils simmer. Cook until the lentils are just tender, 7 to 10 minutes. Drain the lentils and transfer them to a mixing bowl.

5   Place the butter in a skillet and melt it over medium-high heat. Add the shallot and quince and cook, stirring frequently, until they have softened, about 10 minutes. Transfer the mixture to the mixing bowl with the lentils. Add the sugar, curry, cumin, and cider and stir until thoroughly combined.

6   Stuff the beets with the lentil mixture, season with the remaining salt and pepper, and return the pan to the oven. Roast until the beets reach the desired level of tenderness, 15 to 20 minutes.

7   Remove the pan from the oven, garnish the stuffed beets with thyme, and serve.

Paella Tomatoes

3 tablespoons extra-virgin olive oil

2 garlic cloves, minced

1 cup medium-grain rice, rinsed well and drained

½ cup dry white wine

1 cup Vegetable Stock (see page 233)

⅛ teaspoon saffron threads

¼ cup peas

½ cup mixed frozen shrimp and calamari

8 small tomatoes

1 teaspoon kosher salt

½ teaspoon black pepper

1 Preheat the oven to 400°F. Place 1 tablespoon of olive oil in a large skillet and warm it over medium-high heat. Add the garlic and cook, stirring continually, for 1 minute. Stir in the rice, wine, stock, and saffron, cover the pan, and simmer for 10 minutes.

2 Stir in the peas and seafood and cook until the seafood is almost cooked through, 3 to 4 minutes.

3 Rinse the tomatoes, cut off their tops, and scoop out the pulp. Set the tops aside and reserve the pulp for another preparation. Place the hollowed-out tomatoes on a sheet pan.

4 Season the paella with the salt and pepper and then spoon it into the hollowed-out tomatoes.

5 Place the tops back on the stuffed tomatoes and drizzle the remaining olive oil over them. Place the stuffed tomatoes in the oven and bake until they are tender, 15 to 20 minutes.

6 Remove the stuffed tomatoes from the oven and serve.

Eggplant with Cherry Tomatoes & Figs

2 eggplants, halved lengthwise

1 tablespoon extra-virgin olive oil

1 teaspoon kosher salt

2 figs, sliced

¼ cup sliced cherry tomatoes

1 teaspoon chia seeds

½ cup plain yogurt

Fresh parsley, chopped, for garnish

Leeks, rinsed well and sliced, for garnish

1   Preheat the oven to 350°F. Place the eggplants on a sheet pan, cut side up, drizzle the olive oil over them, and season with the salt. Place the eggplants in the oven and roast until they start to collapse, 30 to 40 minutes.

2   Remove the sheet pan from the oven and layer the sliced figs and tomatoes on top of the eggplants.

3   Set the oven's broiler to high and place the sheet pan under the broiler. Broil until the figs start to caramelize, about 5 minutes.

4   Remove the pan from the oven, combine the chia seeds and yogurt, and then top the eggplants with dollops of the mixture. Garnish with parsley and leeks and serve immediately.

Appendix

Yield: 6 Cups | Active Time: 20 Minutes | Total Time: 3 Hours

Vegetable Stock

2 tablespoons extra-virgin olive oil

2 large leeks, trimmed and rinsed well

2 large carrots, peeled and sliced

2 celery stalks, sliced

2 large yellow onions, sliced

3 garlic cloves, unpeeled but smashed

2 sprigs of fresh parsley

2 sprigs of fresh thyme

1 bay leaf

8 cups water

½ teaspoon black peppercorns

Salt, to taste

1   Place the olive oil and the vegetables in a large stockpot and cook over low heat until the liquid they release has evaporated. This will allow the flavor of the vegetables to become concentrated.

2   Add the garlic, parsley, thyme, bay leaf, water, peppercorns, and salt. Raise the heat to high and bring to a boil. Reduce the heat so that the stock simmers and cook for 2 hours, while skimming to remove any impurities that float to the surface.

3   Strain through a fine sieve, let the stock cool slightly, and place in the refrigerator, uncovered, to chill. Remove the fat layer and cover the stock. The stock will keep in the refrigerator for 3 to 5 days, and in the freezer for up to 3 months.

Chicken Stock

5 lbs. leftover chicken bones

16 cups cold water

¼ cup white wine

1 onion, chopped

1 celery stalk, chopped

1 carrot, chopped

2 bay leaves

10 sprigs of fresh parsley

10 sprigs of fresh thyme

1 teaspoon black peppercorns

Salt, to taste

1   Preheat the oven to 400°F. Place the chicken bones on a sheet pan, place them in the oven, and roast them until they are caramelized, about 1 hour.

2   Remove the chicken bones from the oven and place them in a stockpot. Cover them with the water and bring to a boil, skimming to remove any impurities that rise to the surface.

3   Deglaze the sheet pan with the white wine, scraping up any browned bits from the bottom. Stir the liquid into the stock, add the remaining ingredients, and reduce the heat so that the stock simmers. Simmer the stock until it has reduced by three-quarters and the flavor is to your liking, about 6 hours, skimming the surface as needed.

4   Strain the stock and either use immediately or let it cool completely before storing it in the refrigerator.

Pesto

2 cups packed fresh basil leaves

1 cup packed fresh baby spinach

2 cups freshly grated Parmesan cheese

¼ cup pine nuts

1 garlic clove

2 teaspoons fresh lemon juice

Salt and pepper, to taste

½ cup extra-virgin olive oil

1   Place all of the ingredients, except for the olive oil, in a food processor and pulse until pureed.

2   Transfer the puree to a mixing bowl. While whisking, add the olive oil in a slow stream until it is emulsified. Use immediately or store in the refrigerator.

Hard-Boiled Eggs

8 large eggs

1 Prepare an ice bath. Place the eggs in a saucepan large enough that they can sit on the bottom in a single layer. Cover with 1 inch of cold water and bring to a boil over high heat.

2 Remove the saucepan from heat, cover, and let the eggs stand for 12 minutes.

3 Drain the eggs and place them in the ice bath until they are completely chilled. Peel the eggs and enjoy.

Yield: 8 Cups | Active Time: 1 Hour | Total Time: 10 Hours

Beef Stock

2 lbs. yellow onions, chopped

1 lb. carrots, chopped

1 lb. celery, chopped

5 lbs. beef bones

2 tablespoons tomato paste

16 cups water

1 cup red wine

1 tablespoon black peppercorns

2 bay leaves

3 sprigs of fresh thyme

3 sprigs of fresh parsley

1 Preheat the oven to 375°F. Divide the onions, carrots, and celery among two sheet pans in even layers. Place the beef bones on top, place the pans in the oven, and roast the vegetables and beef bones for 45 minutes.

2 Spread the tomato paste over the beef bones and then roast for another 5 minutes.

3 Remove the pans from the oven, transfer the vegetables and beef bones to a stockpot, and cover with the water. Bring to a boil.

4 Reduce the heat so that the stock simmers. Deglaze the sheet pans with the red wine, scraping up any browned bits from the bottom. Stir the liquid into the stock, add the remaining ingredients, and cook, skimming any impurities that rise to the surface, until the stock has reduced by half and the flavor is to your liking, about 6 hours.

5 Strain the stock and either use immediately or let it cool completely before storing in the refrigerator.

Béchamel Sauce

4 tablespoons unsalted butter

¼ cup all-purpose flour

2 cups whole milk

¼ teaspoon freshly grated nutmeg

Salt and pepper, to taste

1 Place the butter in a medium saucepan and melt it over medium heat. Add the flour and cook, stirring continually, for 5 minutes, until the mixture turns golden brown.

2 Add ½ cup of the milk and stir vigorously until the mixture has thinned somewhat. Add the remaining milk and cook, stirring continually, until the mixture starts to thicken.

3 Stir in the nutmeg, season the sauce with salt and pepper, and use immediately or store in the refrigerator.

Yield: 1½ Cups | Active Time: 5 Minutes | Total Time: 5 Minutes

Green Goddess Dressing

½ cup mayonnaise

⅔ cup buttermilk

1 tablespoon fresh lemon juice

2 tablespoons chopped celery leaves

2 tablespoons chopped fresh parsley

2 tablespoons chopped fresh tarragon

2 tablespoons sliced fresh chives

2 teaspoons kosher salt

1 teaspoon black pepper

Place all of the ingredients in a food processor, blitz until smooth, and use immediately or store in the refrigerator.

Chimichurri Sauce

1 cup fresh parsley

2 large garlic cloves, smashed

1 teaspoon dried thyme

¼ teaspoon red pepper flakes

½ cup water

¼ cup white wine vinegar

¼ cup extra-virgin olive oil

1 teaspoon fine sea salt

⅛ teaspoon black pepper

1   Use a mortar and pestle or a food processor to combine the ingredients until the sauce has the desired texture. Use immediately or store in the refrigerator.

Yield: 1 Cup | Active Time: 20 Minutes | Total Time: 1 Hour

Smoky Relish

4 tablespoons unsalted butter

1 small yellow onion, finely chopped

1 red apple, cored and finely diced

2 tablespoon raisins

2 tablespoons brown sugar

2 tablespoons apple cider vinegar

2 tablespoons BBQ sauce

½ teaspoon smoked paprika

1 Place the butter in a small saucepan and melt it over medium heat. Add the onion and cook, stirring occasionally, until it starts to soften, about 5 minutes.

2 Add the remaining ingredients and bring to a boil. Reduce the heat to medium-low and simmer the relish until it has thickened, 8 to 10 minutes. Remove the pan from heat and let the relish cool before serving or storing in the refrigerator.

Pistachio Gremolata

½ cup finely chopped fresh cilantro

¼ cup finely chopped salted pistachios

2 garlic cloves, minced

Zest and juice of 1 lemon

1   Place all of the ingredients in a mixing bowl and stir until thoroughly combined. Use immediately or store in the refrigerator.

Tapenade

3 cups pitted Kalamata olives

1 tablespoon extra-virgin olive oil

1 tablespoon balsamic vinegar

2 garlic cloves, grated

Place all of the ingredients in a food processor and pulse until the mixture is a chunky puree. Use immediately or store in the refrigerator.

Fig & Rhubarb Compote

1 tablespoon extra-virgin olive oil

1 shallot, diced

4 rhubarb stalks, cut into 1-inch-thick pieces

½ cup quartered dried figs

3 tablespoons brown sugar

2 tablespoons red wine vinegar

1 Place the olive oil in a large skillet and warm it over medium heat. Add the shallot and cook, stirring occasionally, until it has softened, about 5 minutes.

2 Add the rhubarb, figs, brown sugar, and vinegar and cook, stirring occasionally, until the compote has thickened, 8 to 10 minutes. Remove the pan from heat and let the compote cool completely before serving or storing in the refrigerator.

Lemon & Tahini Dressing

¾ cup full-fat Greek yogurt

1 garlic clove, minced

2 tablespoons tahini paste

Juice of 1 lemon

½ teaspoon cumin

Salt and pepper, to taste

1 tablespoon extra-virgin olive oil

1   Place the yogurt, garlic, tahini, lemon juice, and cumin in a small bowl and whisk to combine.

2   Season the sauce with salt and pepper, add the olive oil, and whisk until incorporated. Use immediately or store in the refrigerator.

Aioli

2 large egg yolks

2 teaspoons Dijon mustard

2 teaspoons fresh lemon juice

1 garlic clove, minced

¾ cup canola oil

¼ cup extra-virgin olive oil

Salt and pepper, to taste

1 Place the egg yolks, mustard, lemon juice, and garlic in a food processor and blitz until combined.

2 With the food processor running on low, slowly drizzle in the oils until they have emulsified. If the aioli becomes too thick for your liking, stir in water 1 teaspoon at a time until it has thinned out.

3 Season the aioli with salt and pepper and use immediately or store in the refrigerator.

Metric Conversions

Weights

1 oz. = 28 grams

2 oz. = 57 grams

4 oz. (¼ lb.) = 113 grams

8 oz. (½ lb.) = 227 grams

16 oz. (1 lb.) = 454 grams

Volume Measures

⅛ teaspoon = 0.6 ml

¼ teaspoon = 1.23 ml

½ teaspoon = 2.5 ml

1 teaspoon = 5 ml

1 tablespoon (3 teaspoons) = ½ fluid oz. = 15 ml

2 tablespoons = 1 fluid oz. = 29.5 ml

¼ cup (4 tablespoons) = 2 fluid oz. = 59 ml

⅓ cup (5⅓ tablespoons) = 2.7 fluid oz. = 80 ml

½ cup (8 tablespoons) = 4 fluid oz. = 120 ml

⅔ cup (10⅔ tablespoons) = 5.4 fluid oz. = 160 ml

¾ cup (12 tablespoons) = 6 fluid oz. = 180 ml

1 cup (16 tablespoons) = 8 fluid oz. = 240 ml

Temperature Equivalents

°F	°C	Gas Mark
225	110	¼
250	130	½
275	140	1
300	150	2
325	170	3
350	180	4
375	190	5
400	200	6
425	220	7
450	230	8
475	240	9
500	250	10

Length Measures

1/16 inch = 1.6 mm

⅛ inch = 3 mm

¼ inch = 6.35 mm

½ inch = 1.25 cm

¾ inch = 2 cm

1 inch = 2.5 cm

Index

About Cider Mill Press Book Publishers

Good ideas ripen with time. From seed to harvest,
Cider Mill Press brings fine reading, information, and entertainment
together between the covers of its creatively crafted books.
Our Cider Mill bears fruit twice a year, publishing a new
crop of titles each spring and fall.

"Where Good Books Are Ready for Press"
501 Nelson Place
Nashville, Tennessee 37214

cidermillpress.com